D1273553

SCALE ARMOR

Modelling the M4 Sherman and the PzKpfw VI Tiger Tanks

SCALE ARMOR

Modelling the M4 Sherman and the PzKpfw VI Tiger Tanks

First published in Great Britain in 2001 by Osprey Publishing,
Elms Court, Chapel Way, Botley, Oxford OX2 9LP, United Kingdom.
Email: info@ospreypublishing.com

Previously published as Modelling Manual 13: *Panzerkampfwagen VI Tiger* and
Modelling Manual 14: *M4 Sherman*

ISBN 1 84176 450 7

Design: Compendium Publishing Ltd
Originated by Acción Press, S.A.
Printed in China through World Print Ltd.

02 03 04 05   10 9 8 7 6 5 4 3 2

FOR A CATALOG OF ALL BOOKS PUBLISHED BY OSPREY MILITARY AND
AVIATION PLEASE CONTACT:

The Marketing Manager, Osprey Direct USA,
c/o Motorbooks International, PO Box 1,
Osceola, WI 54020-0001, USA.
Email: info@ospreydirectusa.com

The Marketing Manager, Osprey Direct UK, PO Box 140,
Wellingborough, Northants, NN8 4ZA, United Kingdom.
Email: info@ospreydirect.co.uk

www.ospreypublishing.com

CONTENTS

MODELLING THE M4 SHERMAN – INTRODUCTION

A BRIEF HISTORY OF THE SHERMAN

The Sherman was the tank that won World War II in the West. There were other Allied tanks, of course, but the Sherman was the one which served in by far the greatest numbers and with all the Western nations. Not only that, but it continued to see battle action well into the 1970s and is still in use with some smaller armies — a record few military vehicles can match.

Work on the Sherman began in 1940, when the US Army recognised that a 75mm gun, larger than any on its existing tanks, would be needed to combat the known German designs in the conflict which was rapidly looming. The first fruits were the M3 Lee and Grant in 1941, which carried this gun in a limited-traverse mount in their hulls, but these were only interim designs while the methods of producing large castings were developed. The Sherman itself entered production in 1942 and proved robust and mechanically reliable.

It came into service in time for the British victory at El Alamein and the US Army landings in Tunisia, and continued to serve with these armies and with Free French, Polish and other Western units as well as with the Soviet army until the end of World War II. After that it was used by many other armies, best known being its use by Israel in the Middle Eastern Wars.

Over 48,000 Shermans were built, and four main hull variations existed. The original M4 had a slab-sided welded hull and used a Wright radial engine originally developed for aircraft use. This was actually the second type into production, beaten by the M4A1 which used the same engine in a rounded cast hull. The M4A2 looked very similar to the M4 but used a diesel engine, and the M4A3 was also similar but had a Ford engine — the best way to tell the M4, M4A2 and M4A3 apart is by the grilles on the engine deck and the shape of the rear hull overhang. The M4A4 had a longer hull in order to fit in a longer Chrysler engine, and so

This is an M4A1 showing its cast hull very well. It is seen in US service during the campaign in Tunisia in 1942–43 and has flat return roller brackets, spoked roadwheels and idler, and the first type of sprocket. The coaxial machine gun next to the 75mm gun has an armoured cover which moved up and down with it, a feature which was dropped even before the wider gun mantlet was introduced.

used a wider wheel spacing. All this was necessary because there were not enough engines of any one type for all the Shermans that were needed.

By 1944 the 75mm gun was clearly no longer good enough to tackle the newer German tanks. British engineers had found a way to mount the far more potent 17-pounder gun in a Sherman turret — producing the famous Firefly — but the US Army did not like this and chose instead a 76mm gun in a new design of turret. The 75mm had a useful high-explosive shell for attacking targets such as emplaced anti-tank guns but was largely ineffective against the German Panther and Tiger tanks. The new guns were more effective against these but had a less potent high explosive shell for use against unarmoured targets. The two gun types were, therefore, mixed in most units, giving them the ability to tackle anti-tank guns as well as tanks. A 105mm howitzer had also been successfully introduced to the Sherman and was quite widely used to bombard enemy guns and infantry, and an extra-heavily-armoured variant, the M4A3E2, was produced in small numbers.

Over the driver and co-driver the original hull fronts had had 'hoods' which were welded into place and formed definite weak spots. A new hull front was introduced in 1944 which eliminated these by having a less steep angle to the glacis, giving room for larger hatches as well as removing the weak spots.

Meanwhile, continual improvements had been made to the original suspension bogies which used vertical springs, known as VVSS, and to the armoured transmission cover which formed the lower hull front, and a number of different roadwheels and tracks were used. The first track style had used plain rubber blocks, but later types had chevrons raised from the rubber and several steel tracks with chevrons or bars were in common use too. Finally a completely new suspension with horizontal springs, known as HVSS, using wider tracks of several types was

This is an M4 in British service and seems to be taking part in the 1943 amphibious assault on Sicily. A deep wading stack has been fixed to the rear to take the exhaust clear of the water and waterproofing fabric covers the engine deck grilles. In this early version of the deep wading equipment the engine air supply is drawn through the open turret hatches which were well above water level; in the fully developed version an air intake stack was fitted to the engine deck. This tank has a gun mantlet which a close look shows to be narrower than the turret front — so it is from a fairly early production batch.

BELOW **This M4A3 has the late, steep hull front and a cast transmission cove as well a the 76mm gun in tis new turret. The HVSS suspension is commonly called 'Easy Eight' as the experimental tanks first equipped with it were designated M4A3Es, but the name does not seem to have been used during World War II.**

developed and put into service in 1944 as well. As if all this wasn't enough, there were several different types of sprocket, idler and commander's turret hatch. And then in post-war Israeli service the Sherman was modified further to produce the M50 and M51 with successively bigger guns.

The Sherman makes an excellent model subject thanks to all these variations, as every single one can be produced from existing kits and conversion sets. The differences can be fascinating!

MODEL SHERMANS THEN AND NOW

There have been many model Shermans over the years in most scales from 1/76 to 1/16. Airfix started the ball rolling in the 1960s with one of the company's first tank kits, a plain M4 75mm version which is still re-released periodically. Later on it was joined by a 1/48 scale kit from Aurora, now a collectors' item, and Revell also produced a kit whose parts were a mixture between 1/32 and 1/35 scale. In the 1970s Tamiya produced a Sherman in 1/35 scale, more of a motorised toy than a scale model but enthusiastically received at the time, and Bandai produced a 1/48 scale model with some interior detail which has now come back onto the market under the label of Fuman from China. Monogram also produced a 1/35 scale Sherman, mounting a multi-barrelled rocket launcher over the turret, and another one came from Nichimo.

More recently there have been a number of good 1/35 scale kits, and it is these which serious modellers will want to find. Italeri came early with a neat kit of the 76mm M4A1, using the late version of the cast hull and the final type of vertically-sprung suspension bogie. This has been withdrawn and re-released on a number of occasions, and can also be found boxed by Revell and by Testors. The second Italeri release was labelled as an M4A2 but was really a quite good kit of the M4A3, and this also disappears and re-surfaces periodically. Italeri also kitted the M4A1 with a rocket launcher over its turret, and if you want to model this variant look for this kit.

BELOW **This Sherman is an M4A2 with the VVSS suspension and mid-production horizontal return roller brackets. Very early VVSS bogies had the return roller mounted directly above them, and late ones used a trailing bracket which was seept upward to the rear. This tank also shows the rocket launcher arrangement, this one an early experiment with short launcher tubes but very similar in appearance to the Calliope type which saw action in North-West Europe.**

Meanwhile Tamiya had not been idle. An excellent model of the 75mm M4A3 with late hull and late vertically-sprung suspension was followed by an equally good early M4. Unfortunately this also comes with the late suspension, but the combination was not unknown and it is quite possible to backdate the suspension with one of the several early suspension sets on the market. Tamiya's M4A3E2 assault tank, however, is not one of its better efforts, with an inaccurate turret and transmission cover and a suspect hull shape. In fact it needs so many aftermarket correction sets that it is better just to get those and use them on the ordinary M4A3 model.

Dragon has also sprung into action with several Sherman kits, which like the Italeri ones are withdrawn and re-released at intervals. Here there's a choice of an early M4A1 with the early suspension bogies, an M4A3 with 105mm howitzer, an M4A3 with flamethrower as modified for use in the Pacific island-hopping war, and a late M4A3 with a 76mm gun in its new turret and the horizontally-sprung suspension. All these are good models, and parts can be swapped between them to produce other versions. Dragon also produces kits of the M50 and M51 Shermans used by the Israeli Army. At the time of writing Dragon had announced an M4A2 Sherman with the late hull front as used on Okinawa by the US Marines, though no further details were available.

Academy has also produced an Israeli M50 Sherman, a slightly different version to the Dragon kit and preferred by many modellers.

As well as the complete kits there are many 1/35 conversion and upgrade sets on the market. Both Resicast and Cromwell Models produce good sets of the earliest suspension, and Cromwell also produces replacement hull tops to allow modelling of the very earliest Shermans. The Tank Workshop has a huge range, designed to fit the Tamiya kits but adaptable to the Dragon ones, from replacement hulls of various types to new turrets, wheel sets which will let you produce a model based on any photograph you find no matter what wheels are in the base kit you use, and even complete interiors for the fighting compartment and engine bay. Armoured Brigade Models and Chesapeake Model Designs also produce really excellent replacement hulls and turrets, and between all these makers you can build any Sherman you choose. Accurate Armour makes a lovely set to allow you to produce any of the four production batches of the Israeli M51 modifications for the Dragon or Academy kits. For detailing there's an equally wide choice, with etched metal sets from Eduard, Aber and Verlinden and accessories from many makers.

This is an M4A4 in British service showing the wider bogie spacing but this time fitted with the solid ribbed roadwheels and idlers despite its early sprockets and flat return roller brackets. This tank retains the narrow gun mantlet and a very close look will reveal the open covering flap of the gunner's periscope sight in front of the commander. The tank is climbing over one of the famous 79th Armoured Division 'funnies', this one a Churchill Ark which was designed to be driven into small rivers or up against high obstacles as a self-propelled bridge.

MODELLING M4 GUN TANKS

INITIAL PRODUCTION M4

The origins of the Sherman were in the T6 medium tank, born out of a series of requisitions submitted in 1941 the aim of which was to make as much use as possible of M3 tank components. The T6 was declared Standard (or in other words fully accepted for service) in September 1941 as the M4 Medium Tank, and generally known as the 'Sherman' in honour of General William Sherman.

The Sherman was the most commonly and widely used tank of the United States Army in World War II and one of the principal tools of Allied victory. Over a period of four years more than 48,000 of these tanks were built, manufactured by Chrysler at the Detroit arsenal, by the Ford Motor Company, Pacific Car and Foundry, General Motors and

An overview of the completed model.

All the figures used to complete the vehicle come from the Dragon range and have been painted with acrylics. The addition of one or more figures always adds a more attractive look to a model.

others. More of these tanks were produced during the war than of any other US type.

The great success of the Sherman lay in its ease of maintenance and high degree of battlefield reliability, its many combat defects being compensated for by its mechanical strength and comparative simplicity of handling. Another point in its favour was the ease with which crews could be trained, a factor that proved to be extremely important during the war.

The version to which this article relates is the initial production M4, with welded hull and typical circular cast steel turret. It was armed with a 75mm gun and carried 90 rounds of ammunition. Its secondary weapons were a 0.50in (12.7mm) machine-gun with 600 rounds for anti-aircraft defence and two 0.30in (7.62mm) machine-guns; one of these was mounted coaxially alongside the main armament and the other was installed in the front section of the hull.

Assembly

The Tamiya model belongs to the new generation of kits from this company; these are very finely moulded and generally accurate. They are easy to assemble, although as always, there is some room for improvement.

We begin by assembling the front section of the tank using the three-piece transmission cover, which is more eye-catching in my opinion. We then continue with the wheels and the rest of the lower hull, following the manufacturer's instructions, which did not present any difficulty. We add a handle made from copper wire to the rear engine access door, once the lower section and the wheels are ready. We then follow up with a layer of putty here and there, carefully adding texture with a thick-bristled brush, without overdoing it, because the effect of mud sticking to the lower sections needs to be realistic.

The upper section of the hull will involve the most detailed work. Firstly we will close up all the holes prepared for the assembly of the

MATERIALS USED
Tamiya M4 Sherman (Early)
Ref. 35190.
Eduard etched metal set
Ref. 35061.
Model Kasten track set
Ref. K-30.
Jordi Rubio gun barrel
Ref. TG-17.
Verlinden .50in MG
Ref. 372.

ABOVE LEFT **Humbrol enamels have been used in dry-brushing to add highlights to the overall one-colour camouflage.**

ABOVE RIGHT **Careful choice and positioning of stowage adds to the realism of the model.**

BELOW **The finished model really looks like a tank ready for combat.**

upper parts, and substitute etched metal items for parts such as the headlamp protectors, tool brackets etc, working very carefully using putty that has been diluted with acetate.

Now we can put the other etched metal parts into place, beginning with the strips along the sides of the upper hull side which on the real tank were used to secure dust shields. We will not be fitting the dust shields to this model. The two front mudguards provided in the kit will not be used since they are too thick, so we make replacements from plastic sheets using the kit parts as patterns. Once these are done, we will reproduce some dents and some minor imperfections, but again without

overdoing it. The mudguard brace is made from plastic strip, rounding off the ends using a watchmakers file. To glue it on, we will use good quality liquid glue with a very liquid consistency, and which has a capillary action — Humbrol's latest formula is very good. As far as tools are concerned, suffice it to say that I recommend you separate the plastic parts from the moulding tree using side cutters, then use a sharp knife to clean up any remaining scars where this was done, and finally polish the surfaces using a Scotch-Brite type scourer.

Once the etched metal parts are in place, we can add on other detail as specified in the instruction sheet, such as the lock springs on the front hatchways, using fine copper wire, which has first been coiled around a needle. We stuck this onto some small pieces of fine, stiffened plastic, using cyanoacrylate superglue. The tools are from the kit itself and from the Academy-Minicraft accessory set.

In addition, the Eduard etched metal stowage brackets can be added to the rear of the turret, replacing the bulky plastic brackets which come moulded to it. We can now add the Jordi Rubio gun and the Verlinden machine gun.

To finish off the assembly, we can prepare the accessories which we will add to the model after it has been painted. The tracks by Model Kasten are excellent, but require a great deal of patience since each one comprises 78 links and each link in turn comprises three sections, totalling 468 parts in all. This means a great deal of work and will certainly require two full weekends to complete. If the sections are stuck on so that the tracks can articulate the final effect is perfection due to its true quality, definitely making all the work worthwhile.

The model is finished in the markings of C Squadron, 3rd Hussars, which formed part of the 9th Armoured Brigade at the time of Operation 'Supercharge'.

NOTE *The Dragon and Tamiya kits can be hard to find. If this is the case or you do not want to tackle the re-working involved in building this model, it is quite possible to use replacement upper hull and suspension sets produced by several manufacturers. These can be used in conjunction with the easily found Tamiya M4 Sherman (Early), ref. 35190.*

M4A1 SHERMAN

The battle of El Alamein in October–November 1942 was one of the turning points of the war, the beginning of the end for the Afrika Korps. One of the factors in the British success were newly arrived Sherman tanks which featured significantly in the final decisive stage of the battle, Operation 'Supercharge'. The initial movements of this offensive were particularly dramatic, as their primary objective was to open a breach in Rommel's anti-tank defences.

At dawn on 2 November, 94 tanks were launched at full speed towards the Tel-el-Aggagir sector. Their orders were to break through the enemy defences at all costs. Seventy-five of these armoured vehicles and their crews were to find their grave in the desert sand.

The Model

To create our impression of one of the tanks which participated in this fierce engagement we use the M4A1 Early Version produced by Dragon as our base model. We start by eliminating the suspension bogies, which we replace with those that come with the Lee or Grant models produced by Tamiya, although we shall need to modify their structure to make them more realistic. This involves adding nuts, oiling holes and

attachment handles or rings, in addition to constructing the return rollers, creating the joins with the chassis and fitting them with Dragon five-spoke wheels with their edges smoothed. We will use the tracks that come with the kit, but file off the raised chevrons from each link, as those on our tank were completely flat.

Modellers who cannot easily find the necessary Dragon and Tamiya kits, or who do not wish to tackle the full reworking involved in building this model as described, can use the replacement upper hull and suspension sets produced by several manufacturers. These can be used with the easily found Tamiya M4 Sherman (Early), ref. 35190.

On the lower body, the one-piece transmission cover indicated in the instructions for assembly has to be replaced with the three-piece type, which was used on these versions. We shall improve the air filters and add a few haulage rings of our own making.

When it comes to the upper hull the periscopes in front of the

MATERIALS USED
M4A1 75mm Early Version, Dragon Ref. 6048.
M3 Lee or M3 Grant, Tamiya Ref. 35039/35041.
Eduard etched metal set Ref. 35061.
Jordi Rubio gun barrel Ref. TG-17.
.50in MG, Verlinden Ref. 372.

How various scratch-built elements were assembled.

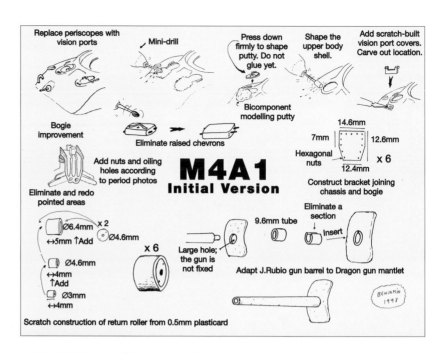

Replace periscopes with vision ports

Mini-drill

Press down firmly to shape putty. Do not glue yet.

Shape the upper body shell.

Add scratch-built vision port covers. Carve out location.

Bicomponent modelling putty

Bogie improvement

Eliminate raised chevrons

M4A1
Initial Version

Add nuts and oiling holes according to period photos

Eliminate and redo pointed areas

14.6mm
7mm
12.6mm
Hexagonal nuts
12.4mm
x 6

Construct bracket joining chassis and bogie

Ø6.4mm x 2
↔5mm ↑Add
Ø4.6mm

9.6mm tube

Eliminate a section
Insert

Ø4.6mm
↔4mm
↑Add

x 6

Large hole; the gun is not fixed

Ø3mm
↔4mm

Adapt J.Rubio gun barrel to Dragon gun mantlet

BENJAMIN 1998

Scratch construction of return roller from 0.5mm plasticard

The bogies from the wheel carriage have to be replaced and improved by adding various elements of detail.

driver's and co-driver's hatches have to be replaced with the hinged vision port covers of the very early Shermans. The mudguards and the tarpaulin for camouflaging the tank are also scratch-built, as are the attachments with which the latter is affixed to the sides of the tank. The towing cable is made from fine copper wire, formed into a coil with the help of a mini-drill.

There is a crate on the front right mudguard that can hold three water cans of the British model, while on the rear left mudguard a bracket has to be fixed to hold an American fuel can. The handles on the chassis are made from stretched plastic, while we also adapted some Eduard etched metal parts supplied for the M4A3. The hoods of the front hatches incorporate some springs that have to be got rid of, since these were not featured on this tank until some months later.

As regards the gun turret, we shall add an improved Browning 0.50in machine gun. The shape of the hatch also has to be remodelled to allow

This frontal view allows the detail added to both mudguards to be appreciated.

The raised chevrons on the track links also have to be eliminated.

Smooth brush strokes create a distinct impression of wear and tear. The brown shades blend in very well with the underlying colour.

for the ejection of cartridge cases from the rear left area.

In turn we reconstruct the handles, antennae and gun shield. The tube for the latter is from Jordi Rubio, while the toolbox is from Verlinden. In addition to all this, we add on ammunition boxes, a funnel, cloths etc.

Painting

During the painting process we did not use any particular special technique. The base colour comprises 70% pink mixed with 30% desert yellow. This shade of primer was then worked on using standard dry brush and oil wash techniques. All the numbers and insignia were painted on with a brush.

ABOVE RIGHT **The signs of peeling paint are distributed across all surfaces of the model.**

BELOW **The M4 and M4A1 had identical engine decks but the tool stowage was very different, as seen here.**

It is very important to refine and rebuild all the minor details: brackets, rings, handles etc.

T.144905

SHERMANS IN THE PACIFIC

The US Marine Corps originated during the American Revolution or War of Independence, in the form of a small unit of seafaring soldiers on the same lines as the British Royal Marines. The first recruitment centre for the Continental or Regular Marines was at Philadelphia but the unit did not see naval action at first — its 'baptism of fire' was on land during the Princeton Campaign.

In September 1776 the Congress Marine Committee approved a uniform. It consisted of a dark green jacket and a white shirtfront and cuffs, changed to red in 1779 because white material was in short supply. Officers wore silver epaulettes. The Marines were disbanded at the end of the war and then reorganised on a more permanent basis in 1798.

The Marine Corps slowly developed into a formidable ground force, demonstrating its valour in the fighting at Belleau Wood and in the Meuse-Argonne Campaign in France during the Great War. Despite this, between the two world wars, it was on the brink of being disbanded for good. The great depression and financial crisis that began in 1929 led to the cutting back of all defence budgets for materials, weapons and troops.

The US Army wished to control all land fighting forces but the Marines did not envisage a role within that organisation for their ground units. They could only survive by remaining an independent corps and finding a new role within the armed forces. Fortunately, a group of farsighted officers suggested that the corps should specialise in amphibious warfare, and train and be equipped to seize and defend beachheads. The Marines would now be responsible for the development of tactics, techniques and all requirements for amphibious combat, and a technical study team was created. In 1930 the Marines began training exercises for their new role. In 1933 the Fleet Marine Force was created, forming an integral part of the fleet, serving directly under the Commander in Chief.

In September 1939, at the beginning of World War II, the Marine Corps numbered only roughly 18,000 men. At the end of the conflict, it mustered 485,883, comprising six divisions and five combat wings, and

---

MATERIALS USED

M4A3 Sherman, Tamiya Ref. 35122.

Top Brass etched metal set Ref. DS-301.

.50 machine gun, Verlinden Ref. 372.

Sherman Update Set, Verlinden, Ref. 0204. contains periscopes, radio aerials of various types, a pedestal for the .50 machine gun, 2 'solid spoke' wheels and 4 'dished' wheels

Spare track links, Top Brass Sherman Detail Set DS-301

Top Brass Sherman Spare Track sets TKA.302 (3 Bar Cleat Pattern), TKA.305 (Rubber Block Pattern), TKA (US Metal Chevron Pattern).

NOTE: *The Top Brass etched metal and track sets are collectors items. Aber, Eduard and On The Mark make etched sets for Shermans and individual Sherman track links of various types are available from Model Kasten and RHPS; these are sets to build the complete tracks for one tank, so contain enough links to provide spares on many models.*

Sherman with numerous spare track links added to the sides for protection. The track pins have been added with sections cut from brass pins.

had developed numerous specialised techniques, weapons and vehicles which were also used by the US Army and other Allied troops. The Marine combat units were deployed exclusively in the Pacific campaign against Japan.

Marine armoured units

The Marine Corps started to receive light tanks in 1941. The intention was to create a battalion for each division, but this did not prove possible until 1944. In the early campaigns small detachments of company strength were all that were available, with the vehicles being M2A4, M3 or M3A1 types. Nominally, these battalions had 72 tanks and 895 men in total, mustered as four companies (A, B, C and D) with three platoons of five tanks each, plus company and battalion staff.

The first Marine tanks to see action were six M2A4 vehicles from A Company of the 1st Marine Tank Battalion which landed on Guadalcanal in August 1942 at the start of the fighting there. In November, B Company of the 2nd Marine Tank Battalion arrived with the 7th Marine Regiment. By early 1943 Marine battalions normally had M3 Stuart tanks, which were soon replaced with more advanced M3A1 and M5 models. In November 1943 the tank battalions started to receive M4A2 Shermans, moving to a normal establishment of 46 Shermans and between 14 and 24 Satan flame-thrower M3A1s.

The 37mm guns of the M3, M3A1 and M5 light tanks proved

Wooden planks were fixed to the sides for protection against Japanese magnetic anti-tank mines. Metal mesh was used over the hull top and all hatches, and spare track links on the hull front. This is a Sherman of 4th Marine Tank Battalion.

inadequate to deal with well-protected Japanese strongholds and bunkers, nor were the tanks well-armoured. The Sherman, with its 75mm gun, proved to be more effective and slowly displaced the Stuart range. By the time of the Iwo Jima campaign, in February 1945, the Marine Tank Battalions had 67 Sherman tanks, of which nine were M4A3s with POA-CWS75H1 flame-throwers using the Canadian Ronson system in place of the 75mm gun, and the rest M4A2 machines.

Frontal protection was increased with spare track links and in this case a spare roadwheel.

Additional protection

Although it was obviously far superior to the Stuart family of tanks, it was very clear from the start that the Sherman's armour plating was very poor, since any medium calibre projectile penetrated it without difficulty. Elements of the Sherman's design dated to 1938 and its armour protected it from the anti-tank weapons of that period, when the standard anti-tank calibre was 37mm. When the M4 entered into combat

Here you can see how the metal mesh protecting the hull top was added in sections which could be hinged up for access to the engine hatches.

in 1942/43, 37mm weapons had been superseded by 50mm, 75mm and 88mm tank and anti-tank guns and its armour was inadequate against these missiles.

From the summer of 1944 on, the Marine Tank Battalions had three new enemies to face: the Japanese Type 1 47 mm anti-tank gun – which started to appear in great numbers after the Marianas campaign in mid-1944, with fatal results for the Marine tank crews, *kamikaze* anti-tank teams, and new magnetic anti-tank mines. The bases of these mines had a system of three magnets joined to ball bearings, which enabled them to attach to any metal surface and when detonated they could pierce a Sherman's armour as if it were made of butter.

Each Marine Tank Battalion therefore started to add additional protection to its Shermans, according to its own combat experience, its imagination and the means available to it. Focussing on the period of the Iwo Jima and Okinawa campaigns, we shall see how various battalions protected their tanks.

The models

The three models we are going to build represent Sherman M4A3s of the 4th, 5th and 6th Marine Tank Battalions in the Iwo Jima and Okinawa campaigns. Reference photographs showing these vehicles can be found in *Tanks Illustrated No. 19, US Marine Tanks in World War Two*, by Steven Zaloga.

Assembly
Step 1
Follow the assembly instructions in the Tamiya kit for Stage 1, detail of the landing gear and wheels. Take note of the illustration on the lid of the box; the Sherman it shows is perfect in this respect. The solid spoked and dished wheels had diametrically opposed screws at lubrication points, which were levelled off. This was achieved using a 0.7mm drill bit and several small screws by Verlinden. The suspension needs 14 greasing nipples at the lubrication points of the roadwheels, return rollers, the bogies themselves and the idlers. 11 bolts of various sizes also need to be added.

Step 2
This was completely assembled only for the 4th Battalion Sherman: the other two have wading equipment and the exhaust pipes are not visible; and the B-11 towing hook is on the reverse side.

Step 3
Very thick putty was used to simulate the accumulation of mud in the lower and side sections of the landing gear.

Step 4
The B-92 part only goes into the 4th Battalion Sherman; in the others it obstructs the wading gear.

Step 5
The spare track links were fitted after the models were painted. The right-hand set was used on each model, the left-hand one only for the last tank. The external telephone box was added from the Verlinden Sherman Update Set. Parts A-4, B-25 and B-39 are not used. The tools are

left until last, when the brass details are in place.

Step 6

Sherman headlamps were removable and the Marine tanks did not carry them in action; they were stowed inside the tank instead. The M4A3 of the 4th Battalion did not have the B-34 footrest — its base requires filing down.

Step 7

Fill in the holes in the front and rear headlamp protectors with putty, putting the brass pieces into place.

Step 8

Use tissue paper to simulate the waterproof covering of the machine gun, which should be stowed on the rear of the turret.

Step 9

Mark and drill with a 0.2mm bit the holes for copper wire to imitate the nails used to protect the hatches, periscopes, ventilators and the commander's hatch of the 5th Battalion tank. The fixing of the wire is left until later. The Marines' Shermans did not use part C-6. Assemble and fix all the turret parts.

Making the appliqué armour

Now the second, and some might say the most interesting, part begins. The Sherman track links were joined together by connectors. Each link has two track pins, showing as four small pins — two each side. The connectors are clamped onto these. When the links are loose, or are at the beginning or end of a track section, the pins are visible. Begin by drilling all the sections with a 0.5mm bit, and insert into these the ends of brass pins, cutting them to size.

The planks are made from

Detail of the landing gear with etched metal from On the Mark and nuts by Verlinden.

Resin periscopes, engraved lids and protectors.

New springs and handles made using copper wire.

Adjusters for the periscopes, lids and connectors in resin.

Padded interior and lock made using etched metal and wire.

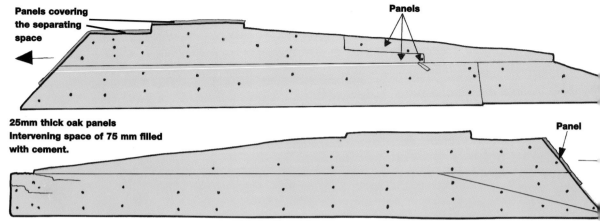

Panels covering the separating space

Panels

25mm thick oak panels Intervening space of 75 mm filled with cement.

Panel

ABOVE **hand-drawn diagram: Size and shape of the side sections which cover the tank, the space between them and the casing is filled with putty.**

RIGHT **Small ice cream sticks have been used for the panels and small nails have been used for bolts.**

BELOW RIGHT **The detail provided by the etched metal is rounded off by the use of pieces of resin until the finest quality detail is achieved.**

BELOW **The deep wading air intake and exhaust outlet are made from thin card, with a coat of clear glue for greater rigidity. Thin plastic sheet can be used instead.**

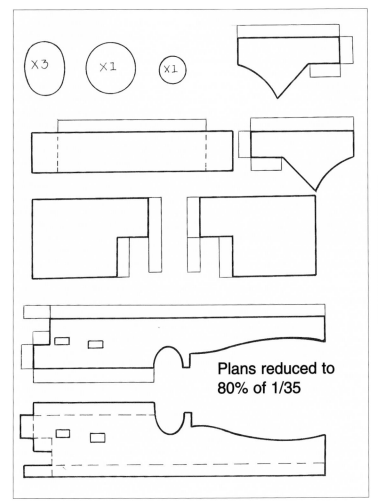

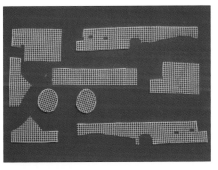

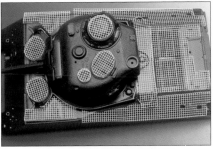

X3 X1 X1

Plans reduced to 80% of 1/35

strips of balsa wood or ice-lolly sticks cut to a width of 10mm. In the 4th Battalion Sherman they were fixed in place with thick bolts. They were spaced out two inches from the hull, or 2mm in 1/35 scale, with the empty space between them and the hull filled with cement which is represented on the model by putty.

The steel mesh is made from very fine gauze stiffened with varnish. Once this has hardened the shapes can be drawn and cut out. The diameter of a wheel can be used for the commander's hatch; and also for the oval hatches of the loader, driver and gunner, but slightly softening the edges; for the periscope the inner drum of the sprocket wheel. Once the tank parts that will be covered by the hatch have been painted, the gratings are glued with matt varnish.

The 25 US gallon can (slightly less than 100 litres) that is carried in the rear contains drinking water: they started to be used in the Marianas campaign, and this is the disposable model used by the M3A1. A cotton reel can be used, rounding off the ends and using strips of paper for the straps and copper wire glue for the hosepipe.

The deep wading gear trunks are made from thin card. They have been drawn as a cut-out, and glued with drops of cyanoacrylate superglue: a coat of varnish and they are ready to assemble and paint.

ABOVE LEFT **Scale drawing in 1/35 of the shapes of the various pieces of protective wire netting.**

TOP **Various pieces comprising the protection, made from net material that has been stiffened using clear glue.**

ABOVE CENTRE **When the material has stiffened it can be glued to all the upper area of the casing and hatches.**

ABOVE **As a pattern for the periscope hatch in the turret the drum of the sprocket wheel is used; the normal wheels can be used for the other hatches.**

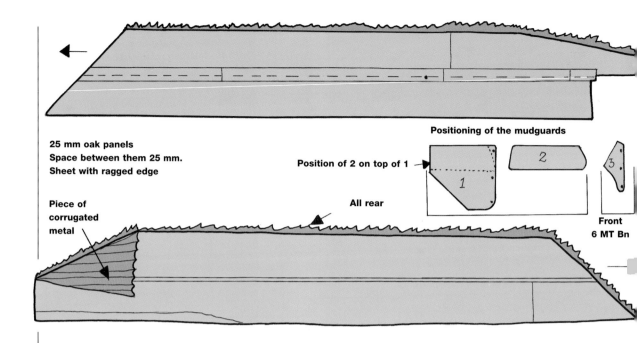

25 mm oak panels
Space between them 25 mm.
Sheet with ragged edge

Piece of
corrugated
metal

Positioning of the mudguards

Position of 2 on top of 1

All rear

1

2

3

Front
6 MT Bn

ABOVE **As well as the planks a piece made from fine metal sheet is incorporated into this model, with jagged edges, with a piece of corrugated metal at the back. The planks are slightly separated from the casing by nails.**

BELOW **To put the planks in place, a small plastic structure is made so that a space is left.**

BELOW RIGHT **Tank made using a filed down cotton reel and detailed with straps.**

Painting

Up until 1945 the painting and camouflage systems officially employed by the Marines were generally inappropriate and most of the time were improved upon by the combatants themselves. When at last some logical standards were put in place, the troops found themselves in terrain the colouring of which was totally different to that encountered previously, so once again the camouflage scheme proved to be unsuited to the context.

The Navy, of which the Marines were formally part, was completely out of touch with the reality of the situation, sending colours of paint that were totally unsuitable. On arrival at their units, the official instruction was that all land vehicles were to be repainted with colour 11 forest green, a darker green than the olive drab with which all vehicles were painted before they left the factory and one that had a slight bluish tint. The forest green contrasted too markedly with the pale sand of most Pacific beaches and stood out therefore during critical phases of amphibious operations. In February 1945 the official specification finally changed: all vehicles belonging to the Marines were now to be painted with colour 3 sand, with patches of earth red and olive drab.

Fate was working against the Marines, however. The little 8km x 4km

LEFT **Note the gap between the
two sets of wooden planks, and
the gap between the upper set
and the hull.**

saddle-shaped island of Iwo Jima ('sulphurous island' in Japanese) was
their next objective, and this was formed out of volcanic rocks covered
by a thick coat of black ash with iridescent metallic streaks. The contrast
between the black sands and the sandy colour of the American vehicles
was too strong, offering easy targets to the new 47-mm Type 1 Japanese
anti-tank guns. Between these and the mines laid throughout the island,
some historians reckon that the Marines lost 50 percent of their
Sherman tanks within the first 24 hours of the battle; others calculate it
to have been 60 percent.

4th Marine Tank Battalion

This unit operated as part of the 4th Marine Division, V Amphibious
Corps, at Iwo Jima. It had been the first to suffer a *kamikaze* suicide squad
attack, during the Marianas campaign of July 1944. These groups would
surround a tank and, while the crew was being distracted at the front,
would attach charges to the fuel tanks, radiator and engine gratings.
Sometimes they would clamber onto the tank and attack the turret
hatches. Their weapons could be magnetic anti-tank mines, packets of
TNT attached to bamboo sticks, bottles of petrol or hand-grenades.

The front hull plates of these Shermans were covered with rubber
track links with their connecting teeth facing outwards. Sometimes
wheels were also attached. They covered the sides of the bodywork with
25mm oak planking, filling the gaps behind these with cement. They
covered the upper section with steel grid that had originally been used
to construct landing strips for smooth terrain such as grassy and sandy
ground: several (up to three or four) layers of sandbags were placed on
top of this 50mm span grid. Protection in the form of grilles was added
to all hatches, while the sides of the turrets would be covered with chains
of smooth rubber links with their connecting teeth facing outwards.

This division was known for applying to the letter an order from high
command concerning the use of the divisional tactical symbol on all
vehicles, as not only did they comply with this but they also stamped it
onto all equipment and materials belonging to the division, such as

ABOVE **Our trio of models, left to right 5th Marine Tank Battalion, 6th Battalion, 4th battalion.**

water and fuel containers, ammunition boxes, 0.30in and 0.50in machine-guns and all troop garments. The tactical symbol of this division was a yellow semi-circle with three code numbers indicating the regiment, battalion and company.

Tanks examined:

Black Jack 21
Bronco	27
Boomerang	19
Comet	38
Coed	40 (flame-thrower)
Cairo	41
Doris	53 (yellow number)

Detail views of the 4th Battalion vehicle.

BELOW **The radio aerial bases are resin and the aerial rods themselves are made with metal wire.**

BELOW RIGHT **Some tanks had an extra container for water, with hose and tap included.**

This unit painted its vehicles in sand colour and olive drab with wavy patches added across the width of the tank with a large brush, plus links and grids. They carried large inter-related numbers and names with the initial of the company in white, so as to offer identification. The location of the number varied according to the company: B Company displayed its numbers on the links on the turret, while the rest of the companies

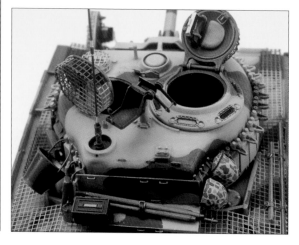

did so on the side planking; the name was shown on the deep wading trunk attached to the hull rear. It seems that the Shermans belonging to D Company were only painted in sand colour.

5th Marine Tank Battalion

This battalion formed part of the 5th Marine Division of the V Amphibious Corps, Iwo Jima. Its Sherman tanks had no additional protection at all on their front sections but they did have 25mm oak planks with a cavity space of another 25mm filled with cement on their sides. To prevent the Japanese clambering up over these, they attached strips of metal sheet cut into the shape of sharpened saw teeth to the upper edge of the planking, while onto the sides of the turrets they fixed track links with their teeth pointing outwards. To protect the hatchways, periscopes and ventilators in the body and turret, they welded on 10cm nails points up From then on, these tanks became known as the 5th Battalion 'hedgehogs'.

During the Iwo Jima campaign this unit suffered a number of suicide attacks, but with a new, more savage, tactic on the part of the Japanese, who now began throwing themselves between the wheels holding grenade belts and explosives. Crews that survived these immediately started to cover the sides of their tanks with planks attached to the three suspension bogies.

The tanks were painted sand colour, earth red and olive drab, but in

LEFT **A good representation of some of the additional protection systems employed: extra track links, plating, nails, etc. This is the 5th Battalion tank.**

BELOW LEFT **Corrugated sheeting with a ragged edge; anything was acceptable to try and keep the Japanese at bay.**

BELOW **The headlamps were often dismounted during daylight hours and stowed inside the tank.**

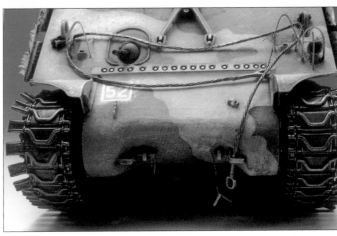

REFERENCES USED

Tanks Illustrated 19, US Marine Tanks in World War II

Osprey/Vanguard 15. *The Sherman Tank in British Service*

Osprey/Vanguard 26. *The Sherman Tank in US and Allied Service*

Osprey/Vanguard 35. *Armour of the Pacific War*

Osprey/Vanguard 39. *US Armour, Camouflage and Markings 1917/45*

Uniforms Illustrated No.11 US Marines in World War Two

AFV No.20. *M4 Medium (Sherman)*

Almark Publications. *American Military Camouflage and Markings 1939/45*

NOTE *Although these books are out of print they can still be found in second-hand book shops and are worth seeking out.*

This 6th Battalion tank is shown with a waterproof cover fitted to prevent water getting in around the gun installation.

a very unusual way: the upper section of the body and turret bore large patches of earth red and olive drab, with only the sides, front and rear of the body and turret painted with sand colour and small patches of earth and olive drab colour. This was all carried out using large brushes.

To identify its tanks, this unit used inter-related numbers in white squares located beneath the hull machine-gun, in the middle of the hull sides, and on the rear part of the turret. Some tanks had names, such as Davy Jones 61.

A number of replacement tanks were given different anti-mine measures. The Sherman M4A3 *Nightmare II* had hexagonal grating attached to a metal frame at 10cm intervals fitted to the driver's and radio-operator's hatches; the track links on the turret were of the T54E1 steel chevron type with the teeth pointing inwards; and nails were only added to the turret hatches.

6th Marine Tank Battalion

This battalion formed part of the recently created 6th Marine Division, III Amphibious Corps, which took part in the Okinawa campaign of April–June 1945.

To protect their tanks, this unit must have ransacked some store for obsolete equipment, for photographs show the bodywork and turrets covered with track links of various types. Each crew attached these links in a different manner, according to taste and personal preference. To provide protection for the sides of the vehicles, they welded strips of iron on between the wheel carriages, reinforced in some instances with sheeting.

The identification system was a copy of the British one: geometric shapes containing the number of the tank, all in white. When numerous track sections had been fitted the identifying numbers could be obscured so some crews cut out squares of sheeting, welded these to the links and painted their identification symbols on them.

The tanks were painted a sand colour with large wavy patches of earth red,and the track links were very rusty bare steel with rubber pads on some types.

As additional protection, the crews of all battalions gave their tanks several coats of paint, throwing on earth while it was still wet, rendering the surface rough and thus making it more difficult for magnetic mines to be attached. Another measure that was commonly taken was the addition of 'extenders', special wide track link connectors which broadened the track to reduce the tank's ground pressure. In this manner the tanks were effectively made lighter when they were moving over soft ground, as with the sands of these islands.

Different types of track links cover the hull front. The ammunition box is folded to shape from an etched metal set.

Vehicle belonging to the 6th Battalion. The identification system involved a geometric shape containing a number.

A telephone for communication with supporting infantry was fitted at the rear.

ABOVE **Here's the completed model showing all the changes made to the original kit. Wrapping camouflage netting or wire mesh round the gun barrel was a common practice in 1944-45; it helped to break up the obvious shape of a long tube.**

M4A4 FIREFLY

There are a number of Firefly kits on the market — the best is probably the Dragon one, but it requires quite a lot of work to the back end (which is about 4mm too long). This article looks instead at a major conversion — almost a transformation — of the easily available Italeri M4A1 into an M4A4 Mark VC Firefly of the 3rd Troop of B Squadron, 13th/18th Royal Hussars, in the Normandy area in the summer of 1944. This regiment, together with the Staffordshire Yeomanry and the East Riding Yeomanry, formed the 27th Independent Armoured Brigade, tasked with providing protection for the 3rd Infantry Division during the landing on 'Sword' beach, on D-Day.

For some years now there has been something of a boom in conversion kits using resin and etched metal, which can provide an infinite range of variations using a plastic model as a base. This particular model has a bit of everything — the modeller has used resin, etched-brass, lead — but at the end of the day both the work and the end result are worthwhile and show well the sort of techniques needed to achieve top results.

The research required to model this vehicle was extensive, the modeller gathering information over quite an extended period of time time. Once he had the information he needed, he had to order the following:

Miniature Armour Conversion (MAC) — Three-part Sherman transmission (resin), ref. 35TT007; Early M4 upper hull (resin), ref. 35TT008.
Top Brass — Sherman steel chevron tracks, Ref. TK303; Sherman etched-metal kit, ref. DS301; English Sherman etched-metal kit,

ref. DS302; Browning 0.50 MG (etched-metal/lead).

KK Castings — Sherman Firefly turret (resin), Ref. KK 06.

Construction

Following the steps in the Italeri instruction sheet, the work was as follows:

Step 1

Make grooves in the rubber tyres on each wheel.

Step 2

Cut off the transmission mount from the lower hull and cut its rear end at a right angle. The lower hull needs extending by 10mm, as the M4A4 hull was longer than the M4A1's. Do this by cutting between the bogie mounts and adding 5mm-wide strips of plastic card between the sections. Before going any further, strengthen these joints by adding plastic strips across the joints inside the hull. Then add the MAC transmission housing to the front of the hull.

Step 3

Replace the Italeri air filters with the MAC air filters, in part No. 24, glue on the MAC box instead of the Italeri box, extending it 3mm. Instead of fitting the hull machine-gun, replace it with the armoured cover which is included in the Firefly turret set.

Step 4

The engine deck has to be rebuilt. Make moulds with Mascolo and copy the filler caps by pressing epoxy putty into them. These can then be fixed in place. Build the raised housing over the radiator with epoxy putty and fill the scribed lines of the Italeri deck with putty too. When the putty has hardened, scribe new lines for the larger deck hatch arrangement. Make radiator grilles with plastic strip and finally add the etched metal light guards and other parts.

Steps 5-6

The driver and machine-gunners hatches are attached to the hull with thin copper wire to allow them to open.

Steps 7-8-9

Assemble the Firefly turret and the etched-metal pieces.

TOP **An overall view of the engine deck shows the changes made as well as the tool layout and gun travel cradle.**

ABOVE **The brackets on the hull side are for 'Sunshade', the codename for a disguise which would make the tank look like a truck to enemy aircraft. As far as is known it was never actually used in North-West Europe, but the fittings were present on at least some tanks.**

BELOW **A front view shows the typical cluttered appearance of a Sherman on active service, with spare wheels and tracks carried on the hull front. The unit markings are clearly shown here, too.**

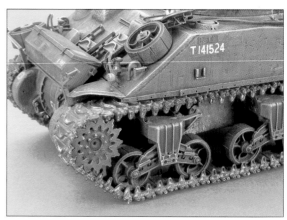

ABOVE **British Shermans, including Fireflies, often carried a camouflage net on this side of their turrets.**

ABOVE RIGHT **The etched-metal light guards give the model a more realistic appearance than the over-thick plastic ones provided by Italeri.**

BELOW RIGHT **Note the air intake grille built into the engine deck, and the stowage box often added to the back of the turret behind the armoured box in which its radio was carried.**

OPPOSITE, TOP LEFT **Netting or mesh was often wrapped around the gun barrel and foliage used to break the gun's outline.**

OPPOSITE, TOP RIGHT **Tool stowage on the starboard side of the engine deck.**

OPPOSITE, CENTRE LEFT **The stowage bin shown on the front was supposed to be on the back of the upper hull. Many crews put it here for easier access.**

OPPOSITE, CENTRE RIGHT **The inserted sections used to lengthen the lower hull will show between the bogies. Fit them flush with the original plastic, and filler used to ensure the joints are perfect.**

OPPOSITE, BELOW **The Firefly looked quite different to M4s in US service.**

Step 9

Assemble the machine-gun and the nine-part gun travel cradle located above the engine . The tracks are plastic, with lead connectors; assemble according to the instruction sheet, and paint with track colour using a dry brush and watercolours to simulate earth and dry mud.

Painting

For the Normandy campaign the British introduced a new Drab colour for their vehicles — Green Khaki No 15 BSCC 987C, 1942. — today available as British Olive Drab/Khaki (Humbrol HM7 or No 159). For the purposes of aerial identification, the turret roofs were painted yellow as per *Airfix* magazine's British Tank WWII guide no 17.

The 13th/18th Royal Hussars used a numerical tank identification system, in red with white edging. the Firefly numbers were — A Squadron: 26, 31 and 36; B Squadron: 48, 53 and 58; C Squadron: 70, 75 and 80. The Verlinden Sherman Tank Markings WWII page No. 347 provided the 'Pregnant Pilchard' brigade insignia and the remaining insignia.

MODELLING M4 VARIANTS

SHERMAN MINEROLLER T1E3

During World War II, dealing with enemy minefields was a regular problem for all armies. All kinds of equipment were tested — from missile launchers to chains and rollers — to clear the mines or enable troops and vehicles to advance safely through mined areas.

The oldest system of mine detection was simply to probe for them manually with bayonets or other hand tools. This was obviously slow and dangerous, and for this reason, even before the war, the British army among others had experimented with various mechanical methods, usually involving the use of either a plough or a roller. The minesweeping plough would be lowered and pushed in front of a tank, so that any mines it encountered were lifted off to the side. This procedure had the advantage that it clearly indicated the safe route to all men and vehicles who followed, but the particular condition of the terrain, above all if it were rocky, frequently caused some mines to escape detection by the plough.

The roller minesweeping system situated in front of a combat tank detonated the mines by the pressure the rollers exerted on the ground, and for this reason they needed to be really heavy to ensure that some mines were not missed, but this weight presented a problem on soft ground because of the tendency for the equipment to become mired. The British army pioneered the use of these devices, with models like the Fowler Roller or AMRA (Anti-Mine Roller Attachment), coupled to Matilda and Valentine tanks. From these the AMRCR (Anti-Mine Reconnaissance Castor Roller) developed and was installed on the Churchill tank.

A South African engineer officer, A. S. J. de Toit, then invented a different procedure, which was more widely used by British forces in the Second World War. This consisted of a series of chains mounted around a drum which was carried in front of the tank. The drum was rotated, powered either by the tank's main engine or an auxiliary motor, and the chains hit the ground with a force sufficient to explode the mines in its path. A Sherman version of this, known as the Crab, was produced and would make an interesting model subject, however our concern here is with another Sherman mine-clearing variant.

The US Army mainly used minesweeping rollers, in three main models. The first was the Mine Exploder T1, based on the M3 Lee tank, of which few were constructed because, by the time the system was ready, the M3s had been withdrawn from the front line. The second, developed from the first, was the Mine Exploder T1E1 or 'earthworm', based on the M32 tank recovery vehicle. This was unsatisfactory because the parent vehicle was unarmed and a mine-clearer usually operated in the forefront of an attack where armament was useful to say the least. Lastly the third system, based on the Sherman, was called Mine Exploder T1E3

ABOVE **View of the completed model from the front right giving a good impression of the overall arrangement of the minerolling equipment.**

RIGHT **The rusty effect is more emphasized on the discs.**

BELOW RIGHT **The mine rollers were driven by chains from the tank's drive sprockets.**

(later called Mine Exploder M1), and commonly known as 'Aunt Jemima'. This device consisted of a set of large discs on axles which were mounted in a frame pivoted on the front of the tank. This is the version featured in this article.

Some 200 roller minesweepers were built. They were first tried out in early 1944 and used on a more extensive scale from shortly after the beginning of the Normandy invasion up until the end of the war in Europe. Due to the equipment's great weight a second tank was sometimes needed to push the one carrying it.. Photographs exist which show the TIE3 system installed in the Sherman M4, M4A1, M4A2 and M4A3, but that does not necessarily rule out the possibility that it was fitted to other models.

The conversion

To reproduce this minesweeping system on a scale of 1/35 we used the Verlinden kit, ref. 0827 Sherman Mineroller T1E3. The Sherman M4A1 has been assembled using our supply of spare parts, and consists of the Italeri M4A1 chassis with its 76mm gun turret replaced by a Tamiya M4A3 turret with 75mm machine gun.

ABOVE **Adhesive paper has been used to make the two rear canvas sections.**

RIGHT **Overall view of the completed model from above.**

We started with the lower areas of the tank in order to texturise them with putty, fine sand and artificial blades of grass before mounting the bogies. The plastic of the kit's upper section is smooth, so it needs work on it to recreate a rougher 'cast' texture. For this purpose we used a bit attached to the minidrill. We then softened the plastic with a solvent, and used a hard brush to roughen the surface further. We added the applique armour plates on the sides with plastic card, making its weld marks with a soldering iron. The Eduard etched metal set provided the headlight protectors, and other parts, which we mounted following the instructions.

The turret's locating ring on the hull needs to be made smaller so that the turret fits snugly. This is done by fixing around the inside of the ring some

plastic rod or strip from Evergreen to adjust the fit of the turret base. The cast appearance of the turret is achieved with the same methods as were used for the hull. The hatch periscopes are from the Sherman Update Set by Verlinden, ref. 0204, as are some of the wheels. The turret is mounted just as it is, and we opted for the older type of hatch for the tank commander, adding a 30-calibre machine gun, also by Verlinden.

It takes time and patience to get all the Mineroller's discs the same thickness. Once this has been achieved the assembly can be mounted, following the instructions, taking care that all the discs are parallel. In the lower sections we added a muddy texture as for the Sherman, but emphasising the effect somewhat more. Finally, once it has been painted, the Mineroller can be joined to the tank with two-part epoxy cement, because it 'weighs' the same as the real one, at a scale of 1/35.

The accessories are almost all surplus parts by Verlinden; except the cylindrical drum made with an Evergreen tube; the rolled canvas is made from gummed paper tape as used for wrapping parcels and the air recognition panel is made from cigarette paper, treated with white glue, and measuring 26mm x 53mm. The small chains hanging from the rear box and those located on the hull front are by Artesania Latina, previously dipped in caustic soda to eliminate their unrealistic gold finish.

Painting

We started by giving a base shade to the entire model with the airbrush, using a consistent mix of 70% olive drab XF62 and 30% dark green XF61. Then as a first stage, we outlined the shape of the tank or recreated panels, adding dark yellow XF60 to the base colour; then for

TOP **Flaking and peeling paint was effected with Vallejo reddish-brown and black, combined with light metallic touches.**

ABOVE CENTRE **The edges were highlighted by dry brushing with Humbrol khaki and green enamels.**

ABOVE **Oil paints were used to give light and dark shading. They were applied as thin washes and blended into the base colour.**

These vehicles transported a wide range of weapons and equipment.

the second stage added buff XF57 colour to the previous mix. To create a shaded effect, we used matt black XF1, very diluted. We used the time these colours took to dry to paint all the accessories. Later on the chromatic variation of the tank was increased, with very subtle blending, using oils in tones of ochre and green.

We left this to dry and proceeded to apply washes in oil in shades of very diluted burnt sienna and black, to accentuate rivets and grooves etc. We finished by dry brushing the edges with Humbrol enamels 72 Khaki Drill and 179 French Artillery Green. We then proceeded to reproduce the flaking and peeling in all areas where this would be likely to occur, using reddish brown and black by Vallejo, adding metallic touches in areas such as hatches and levers. The identification stars are from the decal sheet of the Italeri kit, appropriately cut out and treated with liquids by Micro. The model is finally finished off with matt varnish by Marabu.

Side view of the completed model.

M4A3 SHERMAN CALLIOPE

To construct our model we have used accessories and conversion kits sold by various manufacturers and made from various materials. In doing so we are seeking to offer an example of how options available on the present-day market may be combined, even if this increases the overall cost of making the model considerably. Given that we do not wish to make life too complicated for ourselves, the Sherman Calliope from Italeri represents the most straightforward starting point, one that is more than acceptable, too. It can easily be improved using some etched metal parts together with the Calliope kit produced by Verlinden. We have also used the resin upper hull from Resicast, which coems with cast-on sandbags and their angle-iron

BELOW **Rear view of the completed model.**

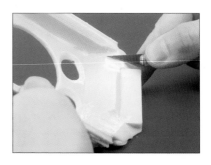

RIGHT **After assembling the bogies, we texture the whole of the chassis, moistening the plastic with liquid adhesive, then pressing down time and again with a smooth brush.**

FAR RIGHT **Reduce the thickness on the inside face of the resin structure by cutting the material back with a sharp blade.**

RIGHT **The upper part of the transmission cover has to be cut away to fit the new resin upper hull.**

FAR RIGHT **It is necessary to check the work by dry-fitting the parts together several times before fixing them.**

supports. These were fitted by the tank crews to improve their protection against German Panzerfaust (a type of bazooka) rockets.

Assembly

We are going to use this kit to combine plastic and resin parts complemented by the relevant etched metal parts.

We begin by removing resin from the inside of the Resicast upper hull. For this purpose we use a knife, eliminating the excess material until we reach the degree of thickness that will allow it to fit onto the plastic chassis. It should be said that the Resicast part is a copy of the Tamiya structure, to which the sandbags have been added, so we shall encounter problems adapting it to fit onto the Italeri chassis. A considerable degree of patience is the only solution.

You have to cut away part of the plastic transmission cover as well to let the new resin part fit, special care needing to be taken over measuring the section to be cut off so as to avoid any unwanted looseness.

BELOW **We cut away the rear plate from the Italeri upper hull and attach it to the resin hull.**

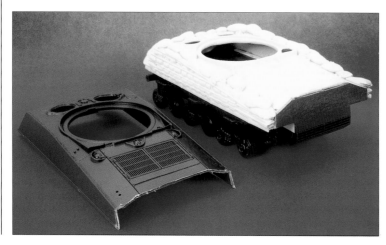

The Tamiya upper hull is longer than the Italeri one, and so is the Resicast conversion part based upon it. We therefore have to cut off the rear plate of the resin upper hull to the length of the Italeri one, and fit the Italeri rear plate in its place after trimming the resin hulls end to the same angle as the Italeri one seen from the side. Once we have undertaken these modifications, we affix the tools, hatches and additional etched metal parts. We need to fit the lights between the sandbags, for

which the hole has to be increased using a blade as otherwise there would be no room for the lightguards. We finish by modelling the sides of the sandbags with putty so that they blend in naturally around the light and lightguards. One labour-saving device is to model a sandbag and place it to cover a light, thus cutting the work by half.

ABOVE **The small handles for the hatches are made from fine wire.**

ABOVE LEFT **We place a sandbag made from two-part epoxy putty such as Milliput to cover the left headlight.**

ABOVE FAR LEFT **After fixing the lightguard you remodel the side of the sandbag.**

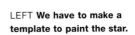

LEFT **We have to make a template to paint the star.**

FAR LEFT **The aluminium gun adds to the clean look of the model as a whole.**

LEFT **A few attachments made from leftover strips of brass and fine plastic are glued on to hold the petrol can.**

FAR LEFT **Various tools and handles are added to the rear deck section.**

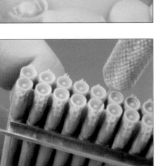

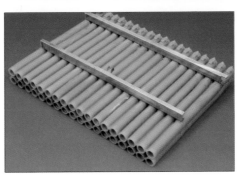

LEFT **Assembly of the rocket tubes is straightforward, although you will need to sandpaper the openings to ensure they are all on the same level.**

FAR LEFT **Using a 0.5mm bit we drill tiny holes into which the cables for the firing system are inserted.**

The unpainted model shows the various materials used.

ABOVE **The base colour is a mixture of 50% dark green and 50% olive, to which we add highlights of dark yellow and buff.**

ABOVE RIGHT **The cables are inserted through a hole located in the right rear of the turret.**

The next step involves assembling the plastic turret, replacing the gun with one turned in aluminium and adding springs to the hatches. We then use etched metal parts to complete the detail. Finally we assemble the resin tubes for the missile-launcher in the usual fashion. We then need to make a few drill holes in the rear part of this so as to insert the firing cables, which are made from copper wire in accordance with the manufacturer's instructions.

Painting

The basic shade of American WWII vehicles was achieved by mixing a ochre colour with black paint to create a very dark shade of olive-green, which would vary enormously depending upon the proportions of the paint, the quantity of solvent, the quality of the paint, the shade of the ochre, etc. Of course, once affected by atmospheric elements the colours would deteriorate and become lighter, then changing and sometimes taking on hues of light khaki or very pale green with various yellowish or greyish tones. Having said this, we are quite sure that there is no exact colour available on the market for a given tank or military vehicle, and this offers us an ample range of options as regards the colours that we can obtain through blending.

Once the relevant drying period has passed we carry out several washes using various ochre and green-coloured oils, which accentuate the impression of ageing in the paintwork and offer a wide variety of shades.

After another drying period, we profile all the detail with a mixture of black, green and dark brown, using an airbrush in areas that are difficult to reach and a brush in the deeper corners.

The highlighting effects across the sides and edges are achieved using a dry brush and a mixture of olive green and cream enamels.

We then paint the sandbags, using Vallejo acrylics: 977 desert yellow, 873 earth colour, 988 khaki, 976 buff, 978 camouflage yellow or any other we wish to choose from this range. We mix these colours together in varying proportions and paint each sandbag with a different shade so as to break the monotony, after which we restore a degree of unity by adding a thin wash with a darker colour and a delicate dry brush coat to mark the texture of the sackcloth.

Finally the tank has to be varnished and lightly dusted with chalk powder in various earth tones to represent the dust which settled upon it in active service.

BELOW LEFT Acrylic paints are applied by brush to vary the colours of the sandbags.

BELOW A light wash with a dark shade in the corners and a smooth coat with a dry brush are sufficient to finish off the sandbags.

BOTTOM LEFT The Friulmodel tracks come as separate links and connectors which have to be fastened together one by one.

BOTTOM CENTRE Use the former provided with the set to line up the sections.

BOTTOM RIGHT Press down firmly on the joint with the handle of a paint brush.

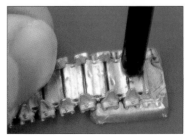

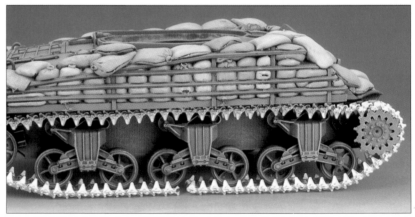

ABOVE **The completed model shows off all the work put into it. INSET The Friulmodel track parts.**

RIGHT **We temporarily add a track link to check whether we have a sufficient number or if we need to add any more. Sherman tracks did not sag along the top unless they were very worn, so don't add too many.**

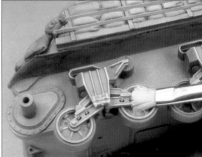

RIGHT **The multi-colour effect of the sandbags adds greatly to the realism of the finished model.**

FAR RIGHT **We dry-brush the lower areas and suspension with a light earth colour.**

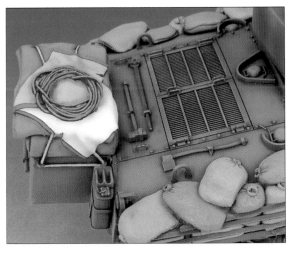

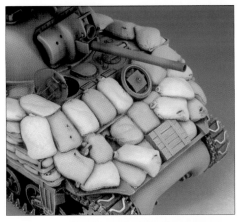

TOP LEFT **Air recognition panels were yellow, orange or cerise with their backs white.**

ABOVE **Finally, we add a smooth wash with earth colours to dull the excessive shine of the metal.**

RIGHT **Between the sandbags is a crate painted with a mix of beige brown and yellow ochre.**

BELOW **Rub the outside face of the track links with a scouring pad designed for metals.**

TOP **Here we can see the black star, together with the ageing effect obtained using washes with oils dissolved in turpentine.**

ABOVE **You lightly dust the wheel carriage by sprinkling earth colour with an airbrush.**

BOTTOM RIGHT **Paint the rubber pads of the track links using a mix of black and earth colours.**

BOTTOM CENTRE **Use a dry brush with a combination of desert yellow and earth colour.**

LEFT **A head-on view shows the purposeful appearance of the Calliope.**

RIGHT **From the rear you can see the exhaust deflector grille carried by the M4A3 Sherman as well as the extra width given by the sandbag armour.**

BOTTOM LEFT **The effect produced when you combine washes with dry brushwork can be clearly seen on the rear part of the rocket tubes.**

BELOW **An overhead view of the completed model.**

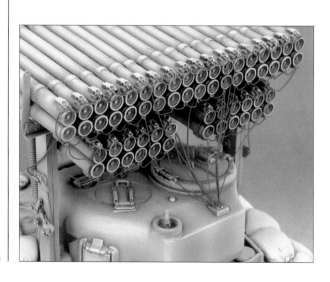

MATERIALS USED
Italeri M4A3 Calliope,
 ref. 288
Resicast Sherman upper
 hull, ref. 35112
Eduard etched metal
 set, ref. 35061
Jordi Rubio gun barrel,
 ref. TG-17
Friulmodel Sherman
 tracks, ref. ATL-12
Verlinden Calliope
 conversion, ref. 803

NOTE *The Italeri kit
appears to be out of
production at the time
of going to press but
can still be found and
can be expected to be
re-released in future.
The Verlinden Calliope
set is also out of
production but can be
obtained from model
shops which specialise
in finding old kits.*

ABOVE **The rusty sheet with
which the spare roadwheel is
attached is painted using 985
reddish brown, over which,
before it has dried, 911 orange is
laid on. This is finished off with
an oil wash using a blacker burnt
sienna earth colour.**

WALKROUND

1 M4A4 with its turret traversed to starboard. Note the short 75mm gun in the original narrow gun mantlet and the appliqué armour welded onto the hull side.

4 The T54E1 steel chevron track, common on Shermans.

2 This three-piece transmission cover was used on all M4A4s and also on all early Shermans of other types.

5 View of the Calliope rocket assembly.

3 The 75mm gun mantlet shows no gunsight aperture beside the gun, instead it has a periscope gunsight.

6 Rear view of Calliope installation.

7 Late M4A1 with 76mm gun. The shape of the new larger turret is completely different to that on the M4A4. This late production tank also shows how the steeper hull front eliminated the 'hoods'.

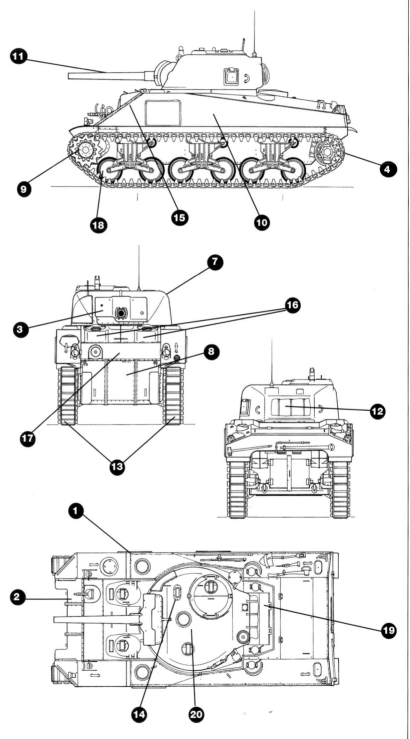

8 M4A1 front view, showing the one piece transmission tower. These had several slight shape variations. This has a fairly sharp bend at the front.

9 One of several drive sprocket shapes used on Shermans.

10 This front view of a late M4A1 shows the hull shape very well.

13 This M4A1 is fitted with T49 parallel cleat steel tracks.

11 Sherman Firefly. Most were built on the M4A4 chassis but the M4 was also used. The long gun is the most obvious recognition point from the front, but the gun mantlet was also a new piece.

14 View from the top of the Firefly's turret. Tthe gunner's and loader's turret periscopes were not in line.

12 Rear view of the Firefly shows the armoured radio box which was a recognition point from the rear.

15 The side view of the Firefly shows the angle of the original hull front on all types.

18 The idler seen here is a common type, as are the road-wheels. This also gives a nice view of the mid-production flat.

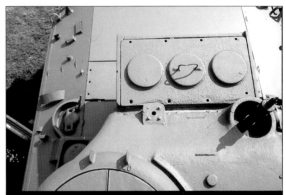

19 This is the top of the Firefly's armoured radio box on the turret rear.

16 The front of the Firefly shows how the hull machine gun emplacement was plated over. This is because the actual gun was removed to make room for more mian gun ammunition. The applique armour plates in front of the driver and co-driver were standard fittings when a tank went through a major overhaul.

17 Here's a closer view of appliqué plates and the deleted machine gun mount. The horizontal bars were fitted to carry spare track links.

20 Turret top Firefly.

SCALE DRAWINGS

M 4 (early)

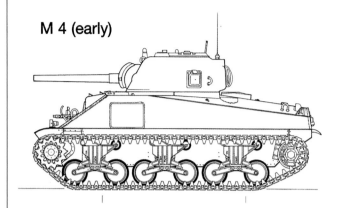

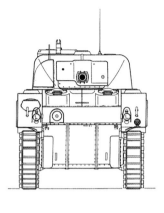

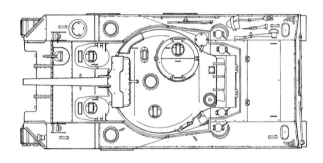

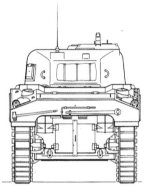

M 4 A 1

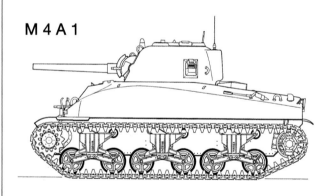

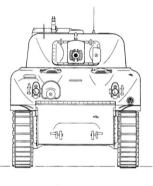

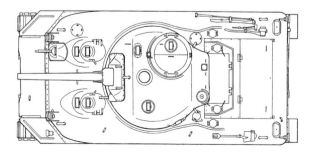

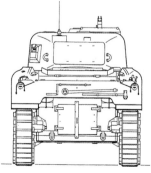

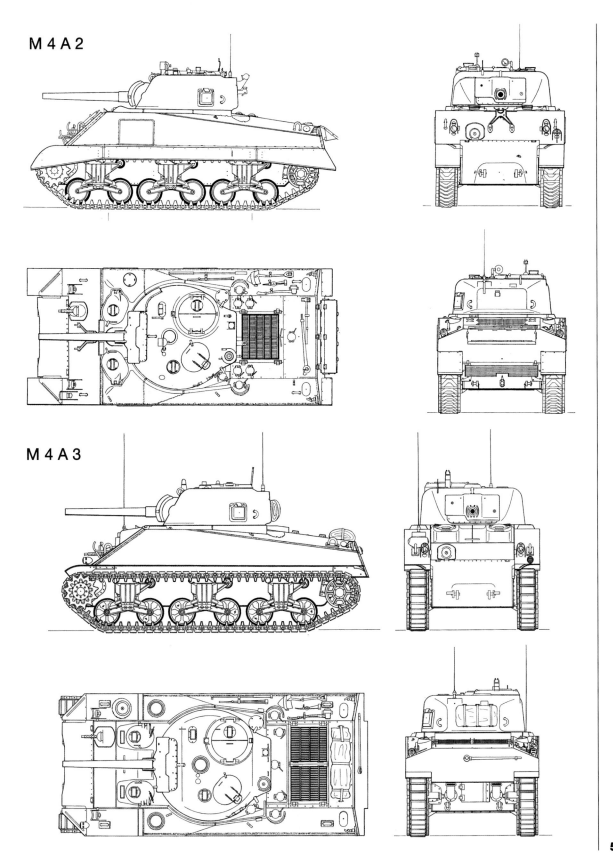

M4A2

M4A3

M 4 A 4

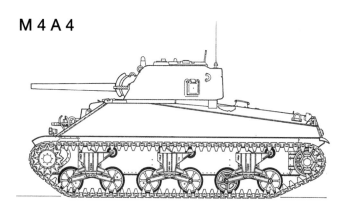

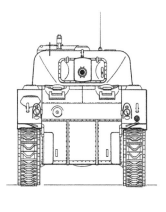

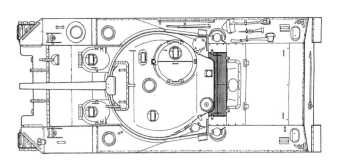

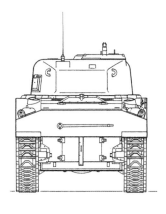

M 4 A 3 (76mm) HVSS

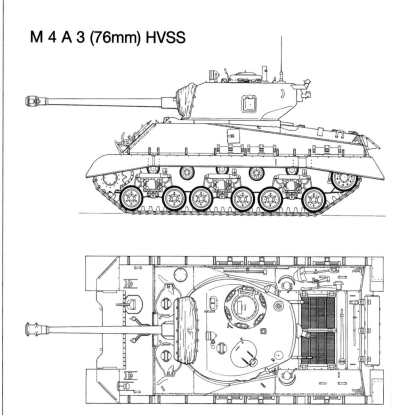

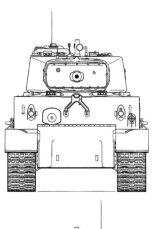

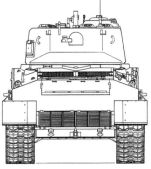

M 4 A 4

M 4 A 3 (105mm)

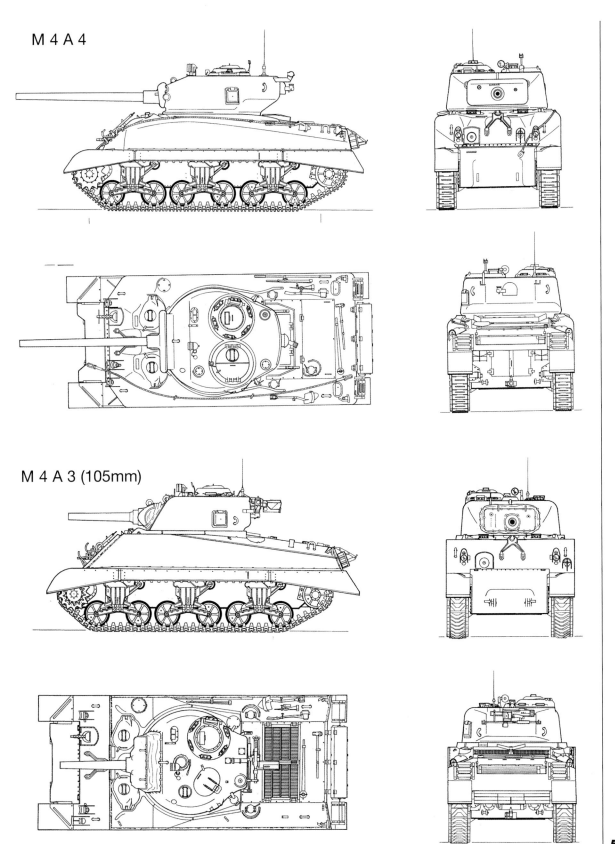

CAMOUFLAGE AND MARKINGS

COLOURS AND PATTERNS

It is a common belief that all US-built tanks came in one colour, olive drab, with no alternative colour schemes. In many cases this is true, but certainly not in the case of the Sherman.

The first Shermans to see action were in British service in North Africa and had been repainted in a sand colour, sometimes with a black

ABOVE **Typical colour scheme and markings of one of the first Shermans to be used by the British forces in North Africa in late 1942. This is an M4A1 of C Squadron, 3rd Hussars, forming part of the 9th Armoured Brigade during the final stages of the battle of El Alamein.**

or red-brown over-pattern. Many of these carried no unit markings but others had large names on their hulls and Squadron symbols on their turrets, and some did carry the proper unit badges at front and rear as well, including the famous Desert Rat sign of the 7th Armoured Division. Next into action were the US Army Shermans in Tunisia, and these started out in plain olive drab though a 'paint' of the local mud was rapidly applied over it when units realised how conspicuously olive drab showed against the local background. These tanks had a variety of markings, many with large yellow stars on their sides, yellow bands around their turrets and yellow geometrical symbols to identify the units using them. Those involved in the first landings carried US flag markings on their sides to show the Vichy French Army that they were not British.

When the fighting in North Africa was over the campaign moved to Sicily and Italy, and here the US Shermans mostly remained in plain olive drab, though some had a black camouflage pattern applied over it. The US star marking was enlarged by a wide circular band round it to make it more conspicuous and less likely to be mistaken at a distance for the German cross markings. Here unit codes were mostly applied on the hull front and rear in the style number, triangle, number, triangle on the left side as seen and letter, number on the right – which stood for the division number with the triangle armour symbol followed by the regiment or battalion number and armour symbol, and the company letter and individual tank number respectively. Tanks under Army-level rather than divisional control left off the first number and triangle on the left side. This pattern was used on all fronts for the remainder of the war, but was not invariable. Some tanks in Italy used coloured bands on their gun barrels to identify the company with numbers on the turret sides to show the individual tank, and in North-West Europe some units applied the identification codes to the sides of the gun barrels.

British Shermans in Sicily and Italy carried several colour schemes, ranging from the olive drab in which they were supplied to multi-coloured sand and green bands with black spots on the sand areas. Those that had been sent to main workshops for repair or the addition of British equipment and stowage arrangements were repainted, and might have been in the standard British colour of 1943, a rich earth brown, or from 1944 onward in the British version of olive drab, a slightly greener colour which faded to much the same colour as faded olive drab. British unit markings were more commonly applied in this theatre, with the unit code number on a coloured square on the left hull front or rear as seen from front and rear respecively and the division symbol on the right. Canadian and Free Polish Shermans followed British practice, though Polish ones tended to carry their divisional emblems on the turret or hull sides and at first had a sand and green camouflage pattern.

Then came D-Day and the landings in France, where the same basic colours of US and British olive drabs were used and the same styles of markings were applied by both armies as in Italy. Some British Shermans seem to have carried a black camouflage pattern, though most were left without this. On the other hand many US Shermans were camouflaged in black, though this does not show in many contemporary black-and-white photographs as it has a low contrast with the olive drab base colour. The star markings were applied to both US and British Shermans, but were often overpainted in black or olive drab as they were thought to make excellent aiming marks for German gunners. US Shermans often carried the tank letter and number on their turret sides, and sometimes a name as well.

The Free French and Free Polish Armies in North-West Europe were equipped from US and British tank stocks respectively, and their Shermans carried the appropriate versions of olive drab. French markings were very colourful with large names and full-colour divisional emblems on the hull sides, but Polish ones were much more subdued and followed the British pattern of a code number on its coloured square and a divisional flash, with the addition of the national identifying letters PL for Poland.

US Army Shermans in the Pacific and those supplied to the Chinese and used in Burma and China, were mostly in plain olive drab with the

TOP **The M4A4 engine deck had a raised housing over its radiator as seen here.**

ABOVE **The typical appearance of a 'remanufactured' early M4, with appliqué armour in front of the driver and co-driver and on the hull side.**

BELOW **Shermans which were to land on open beaches, instead of at docksides, needed to be able to drive through fairly deep water. Small openings could just be sealed temporarily, but the engine air intake and exhaust needed wading trunks as shown here.**

M4A1 of US 1st Armored Division, Italy 1944. Camouflage scheme of three colours:
n° 9 Olive Drab (FS.34087/4F4),
n° 6 Earth Yellow (FS.30257/5D7),
n° 8 Earth Red (FS.30117/7E6).

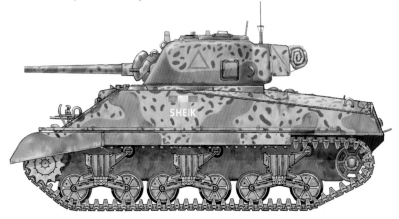

M4A2 of Royal Scots Greys Sherman, Italy 1943, painted in:
Khaki-Green BSCC n° 7.
Light Mud. Blue-Black.

M4A2 at Guam painted in
n° 9 Olive Drab (FS.34087/4F4),
n° 8 Earth Red (FS.30117/7E6).

common marking pattern described above. The colours of the US Marines' Shermans varied from plain olive drab to the two or three-colour pattern described on pages 24-29. British Shermans in Burma seem to have been British olive drab, but may perhaps have been repainted in a deeper green known as 'Jungle Green'. The Soviet Army's Shermans sometimes carried large turret numbers and patriotic slogans on their turrets, and in 1945 white bands were added as an aerial recognition sign when the Allied armies entered Germany and their air forces flew over each other's tanks.

After the war US Shermans remained in their olive drab with the same unit markings, and carried them into the Korean War as well, though here an earth-brown camouflage pattern was sometimes added. British Shermans also seem to have kept their wartime colours, but French ones may have been repainted in a greener shade of olive drab or possibly in the pre-war French *vert armée* colour.

Shermans were also used by both sides in the Arab/Israeli Wars, with Egyptian ones mainly being in plain sand with few if any markings. Israeli Shermans had come from many sources, and up to about 1963 they seem to have been painted in the French version of olive drab. Large chevrons were painted on their sides as unit symbols, but the exact meaning of these has still not been disclosed, while numbers and Hebrew letters were used to identify individual tanks in each unit. The rebuilt and regunned M50 and M51 'Super Shermans' were finished in a colour popularly known as Sinai grey, actually very close to the khaki drab found in several model paint ranges, with the same types of markings.

For more details on all these colour schemes and markings the books mentioned in the reference

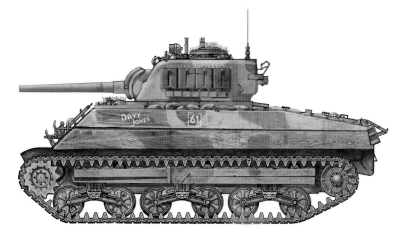

M4A2 of 5th Marines at Iwo Jima. This scheme is of:
n° 9 Olive Drab (FS.34087/4F4),
n° 3 Sand (FS.30277/5C3),
n° 8 Earth Red (FS.30117/7E6).

chapter need to be consulted, as the subject is simply too large to be comprehensively covered in this brief summary.

Sherman M4A3 (76mm) of 14th Armored Division camouflaged in:
n° 9 Olive Drab (FS.34087/4F4),
n° 1 Light Green (FS.34151/30E8),
n° 10 Black (FS.3708)

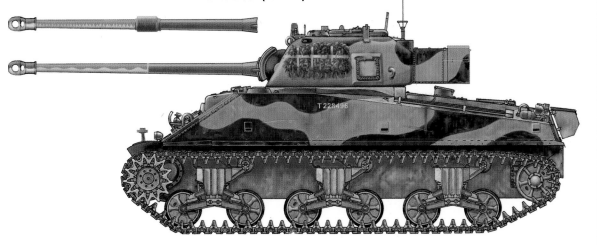

Sherman Firefly of 4th/7th Dragoon Guards, 8th Armoured Brigade. Camo scheme is:
British Olive Drab/Khaki Drab BSCC n°15.
Black BSCC n°14.

MODEL ROUND-UP

Many Sherman kits are available, and even more upgrades and conversions for them. A full list is impossible here for reasons of space, but those shown in the table at right are the easiest to find. Unlike the kits, accessory and upgrade sets can be hard to track down. UK companies/agents are listed below. Otherwise, study the adverts in the model magazines published in your country for stockists elsewhere.

The **Aber** range of etched metal accessories includes several for the Sherman. 35032 is for the M4, M4A1 and M4A3 versions and gives all the basic necessities like tool stowage brackets, periscope and light guards plus other detail parts. 35033 is a similar set for the M4A4 and Firefly while 35054 is for the Israeli M50. Aber also makes 35A35, a set to replace the trackguards on all HVSS Shermans. All are *** A – some experience with etched metal will be needed to handle their smaller parts but they are a good way for beginners in this medium to learn how to use it as each set contains parts that aren't needed for all models and these can be used to practice. The UK agent is Historex Agents, telephone 01304 206720, email Sales@historex-agents.co.uk.

Accurate Armour produces just about every style of Sherman track in resin lengths. These are easy to use, just superglue the lengths together after cleaning them up and use a hairdryer to bend them around the wheels (bending without heat makes resin tracks break). They also have upgrade sets for Dragon's M4A4 and M51 and for Tamiya's early M4 plus several replacement wheel sets of different styles. Rating for all is *** A. Contact Accurate Armour for a full list at telephone 01475 743955, email enquiries@accurate-armour.com.

Armoured Brigade Models produces some excellent Sherman conversions. ABM004A is a very complete set to convert the Italeri M4A1 into an M4 with 105mm howitzer, and gives a new late-version upper hull, turret with turned aluminium gun barrel, and everything else that is needed. The turret and hull are available separately, ABM001 being an early howitzer turret and ABM 002 the late one while ABM003 is the M4 late upper hull. ABM009 is a replacement VVSS suspension set giving the early, horizontal style of return roller brackets.ABM has just announced a new M4A1 hull top with the early direct vision ports and a new set of the original VVSS suspension as fitted to tanks with that hull. Rating for all of these is *** A. Accurate Armour is the UK agent for ABM.

Here's what can be done to put a Sherman in a realistic setting. This Firefly is crossing a railway track, and note how the suspension has been remodelled to show the way the bogies react to changes in the surface level under them.

Maker	Variant	Rating
1/76 scale		
Airfix	M4, VVSS, 75mm gun.	* A
	This is a fairly basic model.	
1/72 scale		
Revell	M4A1, late hull shape, VVSS, 76mm gun.	*** A
	Also available with a set of US Infantry.	
	M4A4 Sherman VC Firefly, with set of	*** A
	Australian infantry.	
1/35 scale		
Academy	Israeli M51.	*** A
Dragon	M4A4 Sherman VC Firefly.	** A
	Available at time of writing.	
	M4A1, early hull shape, VVSS, 75mm gun.	*** A
	Out of production but worth seeking out.	
	M4A2, late hull shape, VVSS, 75mm gun.	*** A?
	Announced for release in 2000.	
	M4A3, flamethrower, late hull shape, HVSS,	*** A
	105mm howitzer. Announced for re-release in 2000.	
	M4A3, late hull shape, HVSS, 76mm gun.	*** A
	Announced for re-release in 2000.	
	M4A4, also available with turret-mounted rockets	**A
	Out of production but worth seeking out.	
	Israeli M50	*** A
	Out of production but worth seeking out.	
	Israeli M51.	** A
Italeri	M4A1, late hull shape, VVSS, 76mm gun.	*** A
Tamiya	M4, early hull shape, VVSS, 75mm gun.	*** A
	M4A3, late hull shape, VVSS, 75mm gun.	*** A
	M4A3E2 Assault Tank, late hull shape, VVSS,	* A
	75mm gun – out of production but sometimes	
	still found. Needs much correction so a model	
	of this tank is best built with a conversion set	
	as listed below.	
1/16 scale		
Tamiya	M4, radio controlled model.	*** B

KEY

Symbol	Meaning
***	a top quality kit
**	medium quality
*	less detailed
A	simple enough for a beginner to build successfully
B	suitable for moderately experienced modellers
C	for experts only

Note: The marking of kits and accessories as simple enough for a beginner is not intended to devalue them in expert eyes, just to show which ones inexperienced modellers can tackle and produce good results from.

WORKING WITH MATERIALS OTHER THAN POLYSTYRENE

Etched-metal sets are usually in brass but may be nickel steel. Either is easy to work if you follow a few simple rules. Rest the metal fret on a hard surface and use a knife blade to cut the parts away, not scissors or side cutters which will tend to distort it. Use a 'spare' finger to hold down the part you're cutting as otherwise it can ping away and be hard to find. Similarly be careful with tweezers! For fixing etched-metal parts to your model you'll need either a two-part epoxy cement or superglue — if the joining surface is tiny the gel-type superglue works best. Use a wooden cocktail stick to put a blob of glue on the part and press it to the model — when the stick gets clogged up, just whittle away its end to reshape it.

Resin is equally easy to work with but its dust is dangerous to breathe, so a few simple precautions are needed. In the first place use a knife to cut away the casting blocks whenever you can; that way you create no dust. If you must saw, file or sandpaper away excess resin; use a dust mask, available from any DIY store. Sand with wet-and-dry paper used wet, to keep the dust down, and always dispose of the dust into a sealable plastic bag as soon as you can. The dust does have a practical use so keep a little in a tight-lidded pot. Resin parts can have small bubbles in them, created by gasses forming while the resin cures in its mould. These can often be filled by using modelling putty, but if they're on an edge or corner the best way to fill them is to put in a small blob of superglue and press a pinch of resin dust onto it. This will set like new resin, so you can carve it to shape and create a sharp edge without having your filler fall out. Epoxy glue or superglue are needed to fix resin parts in place.

White metal is used by some modellers. It is quite soft and easily bent or broken, so be gentle while you handle the parts. Mould seams or the remains of cut-away casting blocks are very easy to clean up with the edge of a blunt knife blade or with a file, and you can use the same epoxy glue or superglue to fix it.

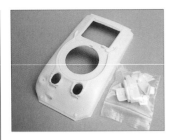

ABOVE **Cromwell Models'
splendid early M4A1 hull with the
vision slots in its front includes
several detail parts missing from
most possible base kits and also
gives the typical British turret-
rear stowage bin.**

BELOW **A typical US Army M4A3
Sherman in France after D-Day.
Applique armour has been added
to cover the vulnerable joints of
the driver's and co-driver's
'hoods' with the glacis plate (not
visible here), and also at the side
to reinforce the armour beside
the ammunition stowed in the
tank.**

Cromwell Models has a very nice replacement hull top to build the earliest M4A1, which had vision ports in front of the driver and co-driver, and a conversion for the very rare M4A6. They also produce nice track sets and replacement wheels, an early suspension bogie set and a T31 turret with its special bunker-busting guns on the sides. Rating for all is *** A. Cromwell can be reached at telephone 0141 402 4016, email cromwell@xs4;.nl.

Eduard also has etched metal sets for the Sherman. 35061 is for the Tamiya M4A3, 35179 for Dragon's M4A4 (including parts for the rocket-armed version), 35182 for the Academy M51 and 35195 for Dragon's Firefly. All are *** for quality but like Aber rated A for the bits that everyone can use and B for the smaller parts. If you can't find them locally, the UK agent is LSA Models, telephone 01273 705420, email lsamodels@mc.mail.com.

Jordi Rubio is an established maker of turned aluminium gun barrels, which include ones for the Sherman. LSA Models is a known stockist in the UK, and other shops also advertise the range in model magazines. Rating *** A.

Model Kasten and **RHPS** also make link-to-link track sets for Shermans. Rating: *** A. Accurate Armour is the UK agent for both firms.

Resicast produces some nice Sherman conversions, including the British-modified Mark 1 Armoured Recovery Vehicle, Beach Armoured Recovery Vehicle and amphibious Duplex Drive Sherman as well as a set of early bogie units. Resicast are at Vieux Chemin de Binche 517, B-7000 Mons, Belgium, fax 32 65 35 18 65, email infos@resicast.com.

The **Tank Workshop** has a host of excellent Sherman sets, far too many to list here but including conversions to produce almost every Sherman variant, interior sets, engine compartments and replacement wheels and turrets to allow simple changes to what a kit provides without going to the lengths of a full conversion to another variant. All are *** rating and A for the simpler sets or B for the more complex ones. LSA Models is the UK agent, so contact them for a full list.

Verlinden Productions has a range of useful Sherman sets in resin. 204 is a basic upgrade set and 263 is a superdetail set. 333 is an M4A2 hull and 341 is a set of US tank periscopes, very useful if all you want to do is add the periscopes inside the hatches which are missing from many polystyrene kits. 646 is a conversion to add a bulldozer blade to VVSS Shermans and 827 builds the mineroller clearance device fitted to some Shermans. 1095 is a radial engine for the M4 and M4A1 while 1120 gives that engine plus its full engine bay and 1136 is an engine and engine bay for the M4A3, while 1244 is a complete early M4 fighting compartment interior. Rating ** B.

Larger model shops often stock the Verlinden range, but you can also mail-order from Historex Agents in the UK and from many stockists in other countries.

REFERENCES

BIBLIOGRAPHY

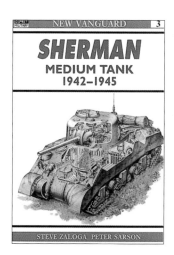

There are many books about Shermans, and one of the best currently in print for a straight-forward modellers' reference is New Vanguard 3, *Sherman Medium Tank 1942–1945,* by Steve Zaloga and Peter Sarson (Osprey, 1993, ISBN 1 85532 296 X). The text describes the main Sherman variants in good detail, clear photographs and colour plates show markings and camouflage of typical examples, and there are even combat reports to read.

Another good Sherman book by Steve Zaloga is *The M4 Sherman at War, the European Theatre 1942–1945* (Concord, 1994, ISBN 962 361 603 1). Here there is a brief description of the Sherman's combat career in Tunisia and Europe followed by nearly 200 photographs and 16 colour plates. The book concentrates on US Army Shermans so those wanting pictures of British and Commonwealth tanks need to look elsewhere. Fortunately there's no shortage of places to look, as Shermans appear in nearly every book on the British Army in World War 2, but no single reference for them appears to exist.

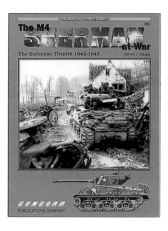

For those wanting pictures of Shermans in World War 2 Pacific service, in Korea, or in Israeli use, Steve Zaloga has several other Concord books. *Tank Battles of the Pacific War 1941–1945* (1995, ISBN 962 361 607 4), *Tank Battles of the Mid-East Wars, (1) The Wars of 1948–1973* (1996, ISBN 962 361 612 0) and, with George Balin, *Tank Warfare in Korea 1950–53* (1994, ISBN 962 361 605 8) all contain plenty of photographs plus colour plates of Shermans in those conflicts.

Sherman In Action by Bruce Culver (Squadron-Signal Publications, 1977, ISBN 0 89747 049 4) has some useful information on the different variants and its in-service photographs include all the important differences between them.

Military Miniatures In Review magazine had an excellent series on Sherman details which has now been published in book form as *Modeler's Guide to the Sherman* (Ampersand Publishing, 1999, no ISBN). Here are detailed sketches of the different types of suspension, roadwheel, track, hull fronts and engine decks but unfortunately the different turret types and guns are not covered and the Firefly is also missing. A modelling section shows what needs to be done to produce 15 different Shermans in US service but does not explain in detail how to build each one. Nevertheless the book is valuable as a supplement to this one.

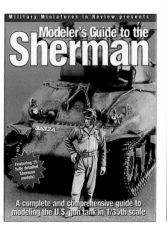

The 'bible' for real Sherman fans is *Sherman, The History of the US Medium Tank,* by R. Hunnicut which goes into great detail on the technical side about the development of the Sherman and all its variants. The ISBN is 0 889141 0805 and all specialist military bookshops will be able to get it, but it is expensive.

Many other Sherman books have been published, some of which are mentioned earlier in this volume. Although nolonger in print they can sometimes be found in military bookshops which carry secopnd-hand books, and it's worth looking around the shelves whenever you find such a shop or its stall at a model show.

SHERMANS IN MUSEUMS

It is not so much a question of which armour museums have Shermans to see as which ones do not. In fact most have at least one Sherman and some have many.

The Tank Museum at Bovington has an almost complete collection of Shermans as used by the British and Commonwealth armies, even including a very early prototype of the M4A1, as well as the amphibious DD version and the Crab mine-clearing flail tank. The Museum library has many photographs and books and is worth a visit in its own right, but an appointment is necessary. The Museum can be contacted at the Tank Museum, Bovington, Dorset, BH20 6JG, telephone 01929 405096 and email admin@tankmuseum.co.uk.

The Musée des Blindes at Saumur in France also has Shermans and can be reached at Musée des Blindes, 1043 route de Fontrevaud, 49000-Saumur, France, telephone 021 41 53 0699, email museedesblindes @symphonie-fai.fr.

It goes without saying that many US armour museums hold Shermans, including the Aberdeen Proving Ground Museum in Maryland, the Patton Museum at Fort Knox, and many smaller collections.

SHERMAN WEBSITES

The prime Sherman resource on the web is Hanno Spoelstra's Sherman Register at http://web.inter.nl.net/users/spoelstra/g104. Here there is all kinds of useful information, and the site cannot be recommended too strongly. Several tank discussion groups on the web are worth a visit, too, where you are welcome to pose questions and get answers from the groups — which include many renowned modellers and Sherman students. Missing Links is at http://missing-lynx.com/, Track-Link at www.track-link.net/, AFV News at www.mo-money.com/AFV-news/, and Hyperscale at www.hyperscale.com/. Genuine enquiries are welcome at all of these.

Other discussion groups and reference sites exist, far too many to list here, but links to them can be found at Tony Matelliano's Scale Model Links, a superb site giving links to all kinds of modelling web resources. This can be found at www.buffnet.net/~tonym/models.htm.

Sherman Register Index

Main page

Activities

Sherman Encyclopedia

Subjects

Links

Update log

Any Sherman related questions? Join G104 - the Sherman Register mailing list

Terms and Conditions

Footnote

Affiliations & Awards

Editor: Hanno Spoelstra

This web site was established on 9 February 1999.

025838

visitors since 2 May 1999.

Last update: 16-10-2000

THE SHERMAN REGISTER
by Hanno Spoelstra

The Sherman M4 Medium Tank series and their related AFVs are my favourite WW-2 vehicles. Over the years I have studied many surviving examples, taking note of the bewildering array of variants and production changes. This hobby gradually shifted into doing some research into their manufacture, (continuing) use and modification. And at some stage, as anyone with the same hobby can tell, one is bound to get their hands dirty on some of them.

The Sherman Register has grown into a network organization with contacts around the world. It is dedicated to the preservation of Sherman tanks and related AFVs in the widest sense of the word.

The goal of this publication is to publish the information which is not covered in mainstream books and magazines. The internet was chosen to publish our research as it is the best medium to exchange information with others and it enables me to update/add pages as soon as more information becomes available. What you see here are the combined efforts of many contributors and myself. Even though some pages are still under construction, they form a basis for discussion or further research.

Please see the index on the left for the contents of this web site.

MODELLING THE PZKPFW VI TIGER – INTRODUCTION

A BRIEF HISTORY OF THE TIGER I

The Tiger I is probably the best-known tank of World War II. Instantly recognisable by its boxy, slab-sided hull topped by a horseshoe-shaped turret mounting a powerful long gun, over its life it underwent a number of subtle changes which make it a fascinating model subject as we hope to show in this book.

German designers were directed to start work as early as 1937 on a heavy 'breakthrough' tank which could spearhead attacks on enemy positions, since it was recognised even then that the Panzer III and IV would be too lightly armoured to withstand opposition from emplaced heavy anti-tank guns of the kind likely to be developed. A number of prototype Tiger designs were developed by the Porsche and Henschel factories, gradually becoming bigger and heavier as demands were made for thicker armour and heavier guns to be carried.

In the end both Henschel and Porsche produced prototypes in the 45-tonne class, and a series of beauty contests were held to decide the best tank. Accounts vary, but it seems that the Porsche entrant broke down more often than did the Henschel one — neither really being ready for the kind of ordeal they were put through.

The Porsche tank was built in limited numbers, and one even saw combat, but most of the chassis produced were converted to self-propelled anti-tank gun carriers. The Henschel tank, however, was selected for production and went from strength to strength after its early bugs were worked out.

All of the early Tigers had dish-shaped road wheels carrying rubber tyres, a plain round commander's cupola shaped like a drum and a pair of add-on air cleaners, known as *Feifel*, on their hull rear plates. Later versions left off the *Feifel* air cleaners and introduced an improved cast

ABOVE **Early Tigers were equipped to ford rivers completely submerged. The turret ring and other openings were sealed, either by inflatable rubber tubes or by screwing down special covers on sealing gaskets, and a snorkel was erected from the engine deck to provide air. This photograph shows the cover on the hull machine gun mount and the erected snorkel — which, despite appearances, is not connected to the commander's cupola but to the engine deck.** *via Chris Ellis*

RIGHT **This is the first Tiger I captured by the Allies. It was an early production version and was taken by the British Army in Tunisia after being hit by 6-pounder anti-tank shells — proof that the Tiger was not invincible. The red turret number 131 is barely visible above the white mark on the turret side, and the unit rhomboid is on the front hull side.** *via Chris Ellis*

After initial combat experience an improved gun mantlet was produced for the Tiger. It had a strengthening rib across the gunsight openings, as can be seen here. This Tiger, apparently in Russia, is carrying barbed wire on its sides, perhaps to stop enemy troops climbing on board — sideways vision was limited, so it was fairly easy for brave men with demolition charges to approach from either side. *via Chris Ellis*

cupola, which was lower and with periscopes for the commander instead of the vision slots in the earlier cupola. The ridged cement finish known as *Zimmerit* was then introduced to prevent the attachment of magnetic anti-tank mines. Finally, a new type of roadwheel was installed, flat with strengthening circular ridges and with no visible rubber tyre. In fact it did have the rubber tyre, but a steel rim was fitted outside it to take the wear of the moving tracks, so it's usually known by modellers as the 'steel wheel'.

These were only the most noticeable changes to the outside of the tank, smaller ones being the use of a gun travel crutch on the back for a while, changes to the mudguards and headlamps, and the omission of the *Feifel* air cleaners. Improvements had been made inside it as well, with a better transmission, more powerful engine and improved turret layout.

With all these changes the Tiger became a very potent opponent for Allied tanks and fought on all fronts from 1943 — Tunisia, Sicily, Italy, the Russian Front, and North-West Europe. It acquired the reputation of being invulnerable as so many shots were seen to bounce of its thick armour. Actually it was far from invulnerable, and the 'bounce' seen was often a shell's burning tracer flying off as the shot penetrated the Tiger. In spite of the fear it inspired, American and British tanks were capable of knocking it out when their tactics were properly co-ordinated, and the later Russian tanks carried guns quite capable of tackling a Tiger head-on with success.

Meanwhile, Hitler had decided that an extra-heavy weapon was needed to knock down reinforced buildings and bunkers when attacking Russian cities. The choice fell on a heavy mortar originally designed for the German Navy as an anti-submarine weapon, and the Tiger was picked to carry it. The turret was removed and a thickly armoured superstructure put in its place, with the mortar mounted in its front. Only a few were built, known now to modellers as the Sturmtiger. They were used in late 1944 and 1945 around Warsaw and on the western borders of Germany, but by then their usefulness was rather limited.

MODELLING TIGERS THEN AND NOW

Model Tigers have been produced in a variety of scales over the years, from 1/76 up to 1/16. Some 40 years ago Airfix included a Tiger in its first model tank kit range in the model railway OO scale — actually 1/76 and the very beginning of this popular scale, though labelled as 1/72 when recently re-released. This was intended to be a mid-production tank, with the drum cupola and steel wheels. A second small-scale Tiger from yesteryear is Nitto's 1/72 model, which came with a rudimentary interior and depicted the early type with dished wheels and *Feifel*. This has also been reissued under the Fujimi label but is hard to find. Although both these were popular in their day, they are only suitable for wargamers looking for a fairly cheap representation of the Tiger rather than an accurate model.

Bandai of Japan then gave us a Tiger in 1/48 scale, again with an interior though rather more complete than the smaller Nitto kit.

Tamiya brought the first 1/35 scale Tiger in 1970. Like the smaller Nitto kit, it was of the early type with drum cupola, dished wheels and *Feifel*. A 1/35 scale kit was also produced by Nichimo, this time of the late Tiger with cast cupola and steel wheels; unfortunately, it had definite problems in its hull proportions.

In more recent years Tamiya has been very good to Tiger modellers, with a whole series of 1/35 kits of versions from the earliest to the last production type. These are excellent models, though only two of them come with the correct turret shape. The Tiger's turret is not symmetrical but actually has its starboard side bent in further at the front than its port side. Kit manufacturers took the short cut of mounting the gun off-centre in its mantlet so that it looked accurate — this put it off the centreline of the tank where it really belongs. However, the difference is

The Porsche Tiger's hull was rebuilt to produce the Ferdinand tank-hunter shown here. This one was captured by the Russians at Kursk in 1943 and shows very nicely the paired roadwheel arrangement and the long 88mm gun. You can also see the impact mark of the shell which knocked it out, high on the superstructure side.
via Chris Ellis

not disastrous to anyone who just wants a model that looks like a Tiger. Corrected turrets are available from the 'cottage industry' makers to deal with the problem for those who want to take the trouble, as listed in Chapter 6 later. Tamiya also produces a fine 1/35 scale Sturmtiger, which comes with a basic interior for its fighting compartment and can be built as an interesting cutaway model.

Italeri has also produced 1/35 Tiger and Sturmtiger kits.

These come with the *Zimmerit* finish which some modellers find hard to reproduce — although after reading Chapter 2, this may change. Although they are often reckoned to be harder to build than Tamiya's kits, the inclusion of the *Zimmerit* makes them a good choice and they do build into good models with care. Italeri also includes a basic interior for the fighting compartment of the Sturmtiger.

A second 1/35 Tiger from Italeri builds the Bergetiger — the recovery variant — which was captured in Italy. This had a small crane on its turret front instead of its gun. It was not actually intended for heavy recovery duties, but seems to have been a tank with a damaged gun which was modified for use either to lay demolition charges or as a towing vehicle capable of lifting the heavy engine decks away from broken-down tanks. Opinions vary as to which guess is right!

Academy has also produced 1/35 Tigers. Their first is an early tank and came with a quite complete, though not fully accurate, interior for the fighting compartment and engine bay; the second kit builds a mid-production tank but does not have the interior parts.

In larger scales, Tamiya produced a 1/25 Tiger with a large amount of interior detail. It had a quite complete, though not completely accurate, interior to its fighting compartment and also a dummy engine top. This has been reissued several times and remains a decent model, though detail fanatics will find much to add or correct.

Larger still are two 1/16 offerings from Verlinden, the well-known producers of resin models, of the Tiger itself and a conversion to turn it into the Sturmtiger. These have had a mixed reception, with some modellers reporting that they are difficult to build. As this book was being written Tamiya announced a new 1/16 Tiger of its own, with multi-function radio control extending not just to turret rotation but even to a 'firing' gun with a recoil action as well as gun and engine sound effects.

MODELLING THE TIGER I

TIGER I AUSF. E (MID): 508th sPzAbt

The 508th schwere Panzer Abteilung (Heavy Tank Unit — the German Abteilung was roughly equivalent to a regiment or battalion) was set up in France on 8 July 1943 from a number of different units. Once training was complete, the unit was sent from its German base in Metz to the Italian region of Arezzo. It is a model of one of these vehicles that starts this section.

The first troops made their way to the Anzio-Nettuno bridgehead. The 1st Company dug in near Aprilia, while the 2nd Company arrived in Rome on 17 February 1944. From that date onwards, the unit was

On the left, number 2, a Tiger I Ausf. E (mid) of the 508th sPzAbt modelled at the start of this chapter. On the right, number 3, a late model vehicle of the 506th sPzAbt covered from page 16.

involved in all combat that took place in Italy. One curious fact is that the Ferdinands of the 653rd schwere Panzerjäger Abteilung (Heavy Tank Destroyer Unit) were attached to the 508th and that, on occasions, the Tiger I tanks were deployed as artillery rather than in their usual role. The 508th sPzAbt also deployed remotely controlled demolition tanks. These were the famous Borgward-built *Ladungsträger* (explosive charge carrier) — the smaller Goliath (Sd Kfz 302) that the unit used to clear minefields at Kursk — and the heavier Sd Kfz 301.

Following its operations in Italy, the battalion was transferred to Germany to train on the new Königstiger (King Tiger) tanks, although it never used them in combat as at that late stage of the war the crews were deployed as infantry. The remainder of the battalion was captured by the Americans in Villach at a time when the unit was training with artillery weaponry.

During its period in active service, the 508th sPzAbt destroyed more than 100 enemy tanks.

Assembly

The Tiger shown here is the intermediate version of the Tiger I Ausf. E. The model used as a basis is the 1/35 scale kit from Tamiya, to which are

LEFT **Minor imperfections — as in real life — need to be shown on the metal aprons too. The plastic ribbing and etched-brass metal brackets can also be seen.**

BELOW LEFT **Detail of the placement of the track links on the side of the turret. Their brackets have also been improved.**

BOTTOM LEFT **In this view from above, the finished detail of the latches for the stowage bin can also be seen.**

OPPOSITE, TOP **Rear view, showing the etched-brass metal grilles.**

OPPOSITE, CENTRE **For authenticity impact marks have been made on the exhaust covers. On this tank the *Zimmerit* also spreads across the rear plate.**

OPPOSITE, BOTTOM **In this side view of the intermediate version, the differences in the *Zimmerit* applied to the turret and the side of the vehicle can be clearly appreciated.**

added a number of improvements — the first being to model the coat of *Zimmerit*. To do this we used Humbrol putty filler, which has different qualities from, for example, Tamiya putty. The drawback of the Humbrol putty is that it is rather more awkward to work with, but it only takes a bit of practice to learn the technique needed for a job like this.

We start by applying a fine coat of putty — spread as evenly as possible — over the required areas (see accompanying photos). To make the putty more malleable we softened it up using acetone and a brush. Next, we made a series of vertical grooves using the point of a 3mm screw-driver for the sides of the body and a 5mm screw-driver for the grooves on the turret.

Once the *Zimmerit* coat had been completed successfully, we worked on the smooth surfaces using a mini-drill and liquid adhesive — to add texture to the remaining surfaces of the tank.

The rest of the improvements were completed using accessories from the widest possible range of sources. Etched-brass pieces from an Eduard kit were used to provide the side skirts, tool clasps, cable brackets and other small items. We used etched-brass bits produced by The Show Modelling for the four grilles and various minor parts. The excellent

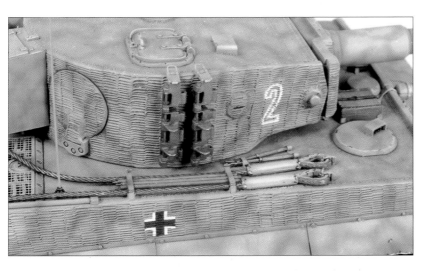

LEFT **The green patches of this particular camouflage come out looking finer and more wavy than usual.**

BELOW LEFT **All the paint work was carried out over an acrylic colour base. This pigment works well when you wish to add washes with oils, dry brushes and so on.**

BOTTOM LEFT **The concave wheels with rubber tyres are a particularly interesting feature of the initial and intermediate versions of the Tiger I.**

OPPOSITE, ABOVE LEFT **Various bits and pieces are added to the front section, following the photographic evidence.**

OPPOSITE, ABOVE RIGHT **In this model the *Zimmerit* has been made out of Humbrol putty softened with acetone. This is done so that the grooves can be easily added with the point of a screwdriver.**

OPPOSITE, BOTTOM **The model ready for painting.**

BELOW **The number on the tank has been produced using an airbrush and a stencil. The uneven surface of the *Zimmerit* means that it almost always needs a little retouching with a brush.**

track links are made of white metal by the Italian manufacturer Friulimodelismo. The aluminium gun is from Jordi Rubio, and we have combined it with parts of the original plastic gun that comes with the kit. The set of wing nuts is from Model Kasten.

To complete this phase of assembly, we reproduced a weld line across the front part of the turret roof, 5mm from the outer line. For this we used a modeling knife attached to a 15w soldering iron.

Painting

Historically this model is located in Italy, in 1943. In this era the Tiger Is of the 508th sPzAbt had an ochre and green camouflage scheme, with single-digit numbers in white without any background.

We started by covering the model with Tamiya XF-60 dark yellow acrylic, applied using an airbrush. Then, with XF-57 buff colour and XF-49 khaki, we brought out highlights and shades using very fine coats.

LEFT **Detail of engine decking and hawser colour.**

BELOW **Note the location of the tools and their fastenings in this front view.**

BOTTOM **Small areas where paint has flaked off have been added to all the surfaces of the tank to add the impression of a working vehicle.**

ABOVE **The finished model.**

For the green flecks use XF-58 olive green mixed with a little XF-5 matt green. For this phase we turned the compressor valve to low pressure and applied smooth, interwoven lines, giving us a very dense form of camouflage.

We left all the paint to dry for 48 hours and then applied a series of very delicate washes with very diluted paint. Later, we brought out highlights using a dry brush with Humbrol Matt Linen No 74.

To reproduce the tank number we used a metal stencil produced by Stencilit. The final finish for the model as a whole was obtained by using Marabu matt varnish.

TIGER I AUSF. E (LATE): 506th sPzAbt

The 506th sPzAbt was created out of the 3rd Battalion, 33rd Tank Regiment of 9th Panzer Division in July 1943 in St Pölten. A little later the unit was transferred to Sennelager for training on Tiger I Ausf Es. After training, the unit was sent to the Eastern Front, specifically to the Zaporosche bridgehead, by rail. The battalion was later divided into a number of *Kampfgruppen* (battle groups) that were assigned to various parts of the sector, where they were involved in continuous skirmishing, both in offensive and defensive combat.

On 23 October 1943, Major Willing — 506th sPzAbt's popular commander, who was held in great esteem by his men — fell in action and Major Lange was appointed the new battalion commander.

To give some idea of the continuous action on the Eastern Front at this time, it should be noted that in the six months from their July arrival at the front to 26 January 1944, only ten of the unit's original Tiger Is remained operational. However, from 20 September 1943 the battalion had accounted for 213 Soviet tanks and 194 Soviet anti-tank guns. The destruction of 16 T-34s in about 10 minutes was one spectacular combat episode that stands out among the others. On another occasion, eight Tigers that had been delayed due to lack of fuel, entered battle and destroyed 20 enemy tanks without incurring any losses. On another occasion, the destruction of a JS-1 tank from a distance of 3,900 meters (nearly 4,300 yards) was documented.

On 29 March 1944 the battalion was once more up to its paper strength of 45 tanks. It continued to fight on the Eastern front, changing from the Tiger I to the King Tiger (Königstiger) on 20 August 1944, when the unit was transferred to the Arnhem sector. Subordinated to the 1st Fallschirmpanzerarmee (Parachute Tank Army), the 3rd Company (15 tanks) was assigned to the 9th SS Panzer Division at Oosterbeek, whilst the rest, together with the 10th SS-Pz Div, was sent to Elst. Both groups participated in combat in this sector.

On 19 December 1944 the remainder of the battalion was sent to the Eiffel Mountains, where they prepared for Hitler's last big thrust in the West — the Ardennes offensive. During this campaign the battalion participated in the battle for Bastogne. After the failure of the

TOP **In this front view small details such as the etched-brass brackets for tools can be appreciated. One characteristic of the final version of the Tiger I is the single, centrally placed Bosch light next to the hull machine gun. Its electric power cable has been made out of copper wire.**

ABOVE **If hatches are to be realistic when open, their inside detail must also be modelled.**

LEFT **This Verlinden figure has been modified to sit more naturally in the turret.**

TOP The cable supports are detailed using small pieces of plastic and etched-brass. These details also show up on the wooden block.

TOP RIGHT This side view shows the *Zimmerit* made from Tamiya putty.

ABOVE Etched-brass grilles and small brackets to support the towing cables.

ABOVE RIGHT Right side view. The effect will be more realistic if the *Zimmerit* layer contains simulated flaked-off areas.

Battle of the Bulge 506th sPzAbt was transferred — without any significant losses — to German territory for reorganisation.

In January 1945, Major Lange was relieved of command by Captain Heiligenstadt, who was captured by the Allies the following month, upon which Captain Romer took command.

After continuous combat against Anglo-American troops on the Western Front, the battalion was left without vehicles and its troops were assigned to infantry units until the unit was dissolved on 14 April 1945 in the city of Iserlohn. During its lifetime schwere Panzerabteilung 506 destroyed more than 400 combat tanks.

Assembly

We are now going to reproduce the final version of the Tiger I Ausf E. Start by thoroughly familiarising yourself with all its particular details — through books, magazine articles and any other medium. The first choice in terms of price and availability is the Vanguard series Tiger I, which gives us the most important action and detail in chronological order.

Another much sought after book in this field is *Tigers in Combat* (see the Bibliography in Chapter 7). As well as these sources, we can use the scale drawings from one of the monographs published in Japan, in particular those in the 'Ground Power' series, to plan out our superdetailing.

To make this procedure clear, we are going to divide it into the following main phases:

GUNS: The kit used is the Tamiya Tiger I (late) — ref. 35416 — which includes a choice of main guns. Our choice was combined with the the aluminium gun produced by Jordi Rubio. This meant removing the barrel and modify the plastic Tamiya version to accept the new barrel. The join was effected by inserting the metal barrel into a hollow plastic disc inside the turret. We chose the binocular type of gunlayer's vision device.

TURRET HATCH: We chose the one with rounded edges.

GENERAL DETAILS: We imitated the welding effects (irregular lines) by using the tip of a modelling knife. The periscopes were made from small 'C' outlines made of Evergreen putty. We made bullet and shell impact holes in the *Zimmerit* by using a circular bit fixed to a minidrill; use slow speeds, and small indentations can be made.

To identify the special details of the final version of the Tiger I, we recommend that you consult the article in issue 41 of *Todo Modelismo* on the tanks of the 507th sPzAbt. For other details we also recommend the Verlinden monograph, which features the tank preserved in the Saumur Museum (see photographs of this vehicle in Chapter 3; here details such as, for example, the cable brackets, can be seen clearly.

As far as the etched-brass pieces are concerned, we made extensive use of various items on the Eduard, Aber and The Show Modelling sheets. As with the model based on the intermediate version, the tracks are from Friulimodelismo. The idler wheel is from Model Kasten and is smaller in the final version.

To refine the model further the etched-brass pieces were used to make wing nuts — these small items are rarely fully convincing in the original model. To produce a more realistic wing nut, first stretch plastic under heat to obtain the finest thread possible, then attach a small

BELOW LEFT **Detail of the commander's turret, which is characteristic of the final version of the Tiger I. The use of diluted putty avoids later sandpapering work on parts that are difficult to reach or delicate detail, and moreover gives a texture that is always appropriate to the model.**

BELOW **The figure has been adapted to suit the location — looking out of the turret escape hatch. Note the *Zimmerit* detail on the turret side.**

LEFT **Positioning of the *Zimmerit* on the front and glacis plate.**

BELOW LEFT **The idler wheels from the kit have been replaced by more realistic Model Kasten ones.**

BELOW AND OPPOSITE, TOP **The finished model ready for painting.**

OPPOSITE, MIDDLE **When reproducing dirt and wear and tear effects, pastels were used, with particular emphasis on the exhaust areas.**

OPPOSITE, BOTTOM **Note the 506th sPzAbt emblem on the rear of the turret.**

amount of thread to each side of the centre, again cutting off any excess.

Other items that need extra refinement include the mudguards and exhaust pipe shields .

ZIMMERIT: For this model we chose Tamiya's putty and the 0.7mm saw-type appliocators sold by the same brand. When mixing the two ingredients of this putty, you have to remember that the paste obtained must reach the colour indicated on the cap of the larger tube. This indicates when the proportions used in the mixture are correct and ready to use.

Painting

The first thing to do is to cover the whole of the tank (minus the tracks attached to it) using the airbrush and Tamiya's acrylic khaki colour (XF-49). Next, taking care not to damage any of the small etched brass pieces, we used successive coats and a dry brush to work with various shades applied with a flat No 6 brush. First we use a dry brush to work with ochre (Humbrol No 83). The second coat is a mixture of ochre plus pale yellow (No 81). The third coat, or dry brush phase, is again completed using a mixture of the two yellows above, but this time adding a little white (No 34).

Finally, we worked with a mixture of pale yellow (No 81) and white (No 34). For a finish which tends more towards yellow, use matt linen (No 74) for this final dry brush phase or cream colour (No 103) can be used for a paler appearance.

If the dry brush work using multiple coats and shades has been carried out correctly, you will see that the model will have acquired a great richness and variety of tone, within the limits of uniformity that the general finish of the tank must have.

The dry-brush painting technique also allows you to ensure that cracked areas and fixtures look darker and that parts with edges or those bits that stand proud of the main structure, are fully evident. Using reddish-brown (Tamiya XF-64) the airbrush is then worked all over the tank to produce faint irregular patches that possess different degrees of intensity, and light and dark.

The next painting phase involves outlining all the areas of the model with oils. For this we used Mir natural dark earth. Later, to highlight the main shapes of the tank and the areas with *Zimmerit* in particular, we used dark brown and

TOP **The final finish for the track links is obtained using metallic paint applied with a dry brush.**

ABOVE **View of the front of the Tiger showing the track links deployed as protection.**

OPPOSITE **Views of the finished model. Note the wear and tear and weathering details — various imperfections such as the detached areas of the *Zimmerit* and the bullet impacts. Note also the realistic finish of the track links.**

black pastel chalks. These chalks were rubbed first on sandpaper to obtain dust and then applied with a fine brush. We particularly recommend the use of black pastel on the exhaust pipes and around the coaxial machine gun.

Whether using oils or pastel colours, the tell-tale marks of liquid trickling down the sides of the tank should always be added in different tones — and should always be done very smoothly. For chipped paint we used a medium grey colour outlined in oils.

To simulate bullet scars and impacts, we made a few marks around where the bullet hole is located, using a little gun metal and silver colour. The chipped paint is produced using a Vallejo dark brown base and small touches of gunmetal or black lead. If the metal colour looks too strong, a little ochre or some similar shade can be added using powdered pastels or an airbrush.

The unit and tactical markings were painted using Stencilit etched-brass stencils. These can be retouched with Vallejo acrylics if necessary — and this retouching often proves to be particularly necessary in areas were the coats of Zimmerit are located.

The metal parts of the tools were painted using a chocolate brown (Humbrol No 98) base, the silver colour then being smoothly applied with a dry brush. Vallejo's white was used as a base for the wooden parts and then a few coats of burnt sienna-coloured oil paint were added. The block has a darker base, in this case medium brown was used.

The tracks are painted in the usual way: a chocolate brown (Humbrol No 82) primer, then a leather colour (Humbrol No 62) wash followed by a final dry brush coat using silver (Humbrol No 11). The entire model was finally glazed with a matt finish, in this instance from Marabú.

A final comment upon the painting of the tank: we would like to mention the red-coloured number next to the letter 'W' that can be seen in the insignia located on the rear of the turret. This letter was painted in honour of original unit commander Willing. The 1st Company used the number and the letter 'W' in white; the 2nd Company in red; and the 3rd Company in yellow. Our model is of tank number three of the 2nd Company, as it operated in May 1944.

Figures

The figure representing the tank commander came from Verlinden Productions, the head, left hand and right arm having been changed. The figure of the radio operator was produced by Cromwell and incorporates a Hornet head. Creating the loader was a more laborious process, although it, too, was produced from a Verlinden figure.

Vallejo acrylics were used to paint their uniforms, with the flesh-coloured parts finished off with oils.

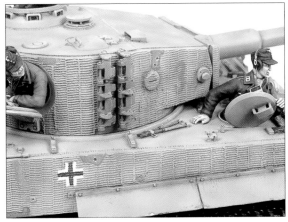

THIS SPREAD **The last of the Panzer Aces — Yoshitaka Hirano's gold medal winner at Euromilitaire 1995 shows a Tamiya 1/35 scale Tiger I with excellent diorama detail.**

The finished 507th sPzAbt Tiger I in spectacular lighting conditions.

TIGER I AUSF. E (LATE): 507th sPzAbt

This unit was formed — by order *AHA I. II Nr. 36817/43 GEKADOS 23-9-43* — from the 4th Panzer Regiment (13th Panzer Division) in Vienna and Brunn (Austria). After being inspected by Guderian in February 1944 and following manoeuvres, it first saw action on 15 March 1944, attached to the 357th Infantry Division, which belonged to the XXXVIIIth Panzer Corps.

On 7 April 1944, two Tigers destroyed four T-34s and three assault guns without suffering any damage. This was the first of many successful engagements on the part of a battalion that, while not the best-known or most successful unit, nonetheless achieved exceptional deeds abounded, such as the series of defensive engagements in the Swisloz sector, in which, during a heavy Soviet assault, the unit destroyed 36 tanks at a cost of 13 of its own. By 20 April 1944, only a month after it had been established, the 507th had already achieved 252 victories over Soviet tanks and 80 over tank destroyers and assault guns.

The unit's most celebrated accomplishment was the counter-attack launched in the early hours of 14 January 1945. It lasted until the 18th,

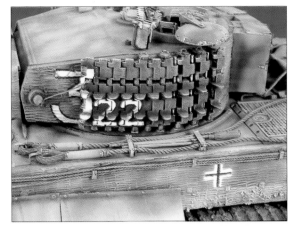

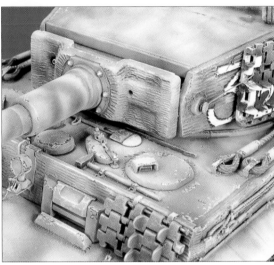

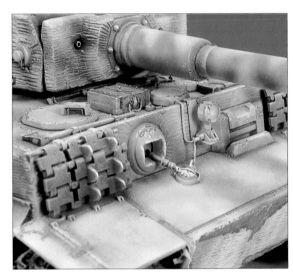

and during it, with only 30 Tigers operational, the unit left 106 Soviet tanks out of action. Although a tactical victory, the battle was a strategic disaster since the Russians, applying pressure to the flank of the offensive, forced unit personnel to abandon and destroy 19 Tigers themselves. It was an attack for which they had a high price to pay as during the withdrawal itself the enemy destroyed another 22 tanks.

Finally, following the battle, the 507th was restructured and equipped with Tiger IIs. Two of its three companies and one of the platoons belonging to the 2nd Company were provided with Jagdpanthers, most of which were taken out by Allied aircraft in the final days of the war; the unit was rebuilt after losing its Jagpanthers and equipped with Flakpanzer IVs and Hetzers. The 507th sPzAbt surrendered to US troops almost without a fight at the end of the war. As in many other cases, the Americans handed over the prisoners from the unit to the Soviet Union, where they spent the next 15 years.

The example we have chosen to model is the only Tiger that was lost during the heavy battle at Szaasy Slotski on 15 January 1945, a tank that, at this time, belonged to the commander of the 3rd Company, Oberleutnant Wirsching, who was wounded in action.

TOP LEFT **To reproduce the *Zimmerit*, we applied a putty base to the surfaces, then modelled this with the point of a screwdriver.**

TOP **The numbering was painted using a stencil, presenting the problem of adapting it to the raised parts and the detail of the track links.**

ABOVE LEFT **The *Zimmerit* is also modelled onto the gun shield.**

ABOVE **Front detail — compare this with the 'live' photograph on page 46.**

ABOVE **The finished model.**

BELOW AND BELOW RIGHT
**Views of some accessories
added to the model, something
that always adds realism. Note
also the dented and ruptured
sheet metal on the edges of the
track guards.**

Model

The work involves On The Mark etched brass pieces, the original tracks from the model, a Jordi Rubio gun and the aluminium sheeting to reconstruct the mudguards. A more detailed breakdown is shown in the drawing on page 30.

A particular characteristic of this battalion was the way it used track links as applique armour — front and back. The *Zimmerit* — as on previous models — is created from Tamiya putty applied in a way that achieves different textures from the rest of the vehicle on the sides of the turret where the *Zimmerit* is thicker and the marks more spaced out.

Painting

Look particularly at the way the unit's numbering goes over the track links that are protecting the turret side. To start the numbering off we removed the links that got in the way. We then made up a stencil to be able to paint the numbers on easily and, once this was done, we put the tracks back in their place.

It's important for verisimilitude to ensure that the numbers are painted on both the turret sides and the track links as this is what was done in the field. The battalion emblem can be obtained from the basic ADV/Azimut decal sheet.

ABOVE **The finished model.**

BELOW **This is the final appearance of the set of wheels and tracks.**

BELOW LEFT **Dirt and wear and tear are always particularly in evidence on the exhaust shields.**

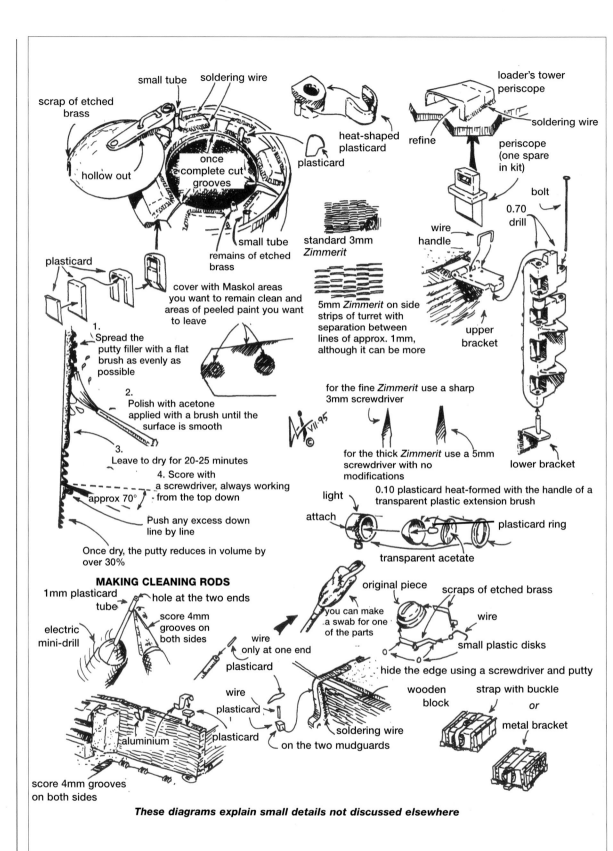

scrap of etched brass

small tube   soldering wire

hollow out

once complete cut grooves

heat-shaped plasticard

plasticard

refine

loader's tower periscope

soldering wire

periscope (one spare in kit)

bolt

small tube

remains of etched brass

0.70 drill

plasticard

cover with Maskol areas you want to remain clean and areas of peeled paint you want to leave

wire handle

standard 3mm *Zimmerit*

5mm *Zimmerit* on side strips of turret with separation between lines of approx. 1mm, although it can be more

upper bracket

1. Spread the putty filler with a flat brush as evenly as possible

2. Polish with acetone applied with a brush until the surface is smooth

3. Leave to dry for 20-25 minutes

4. Score with a screwdriver, always working from the top down

approx 70°

Push any excess down line by line

Once dry, the putty reduces in volume by over 30%

for the fine *Zimmerit* use a sharp 3mm screwdriver

for the thick *Zimmerit* use a 5mm screwdriver with no modifications

lower bracket

light

attach

0.10 plasticard heat-formed with the handle of a transparent plastic extension brush

plasticard ring

transparent acetate

MAKING CLEANING RODS

1mm plasticard tube

hole at the two ends

electric mini-drill

score 4mm grooves on both sides

wire only at one end

plasticard

wire

plasticard

plasticard

aluminium

score 4mm grooves on both sides

original piece

you can make a swab for one of the parts

scraps of etched brass

wire

small plastic disks

hide the edge using a screwdriver and putty

wooden block

strap with buckle

or

metal bracket

soldering wire on the two mudguards

These diagrams explain small details not discussed elsewhere

LATE MODEL TIGER I

This Tiger tank model is from Tamiya — it does not need changing, it is very good as it stands, but it can be markedly improved by superdetailing. The model detail is complemented with etched-brass parts made by On The Mark, and specific improvements have been made to many other parts. For example, the mudguards have been refined, the towing cables have been changed for home-made ones and the plastic levers have been exchanged for ones made of wire; additionally, all over the tank we have added the characteristic welding marks. The tracks are assembled from Model Kasten links, one by one — an unbeatable, if slow, method but one that really pays off in the finished result. The addition of *Zimmerit* to all the vertical surfaces of the vehicle is an absolute requirement for the Tiger. For this model it has been added using a 17w soldering iron, to which the appropriate blade was attached.

Painting

An airbrush, a dry brush and lots of washes were used for the painting. The airbrush is used to apply the base coat and to highlight and emphasise the shape of the tank, shading in the hollows and thinning down flat areas.

The dry brush technique was used to make ridges and other smaller details stand out. Using washes with dark colours, we outlined all the rivets, screws, handles, hatches and so on in a distinctive and individual manner so as to help all the detail to stand out. In addition, the latter technique is highly suitable for painting the muddy bits of the Tiger, grease marks, fuel stains, areas of rust and so on.

The Tiger sports a camouflage pattern consisting of the three standard colours used by the German army from 1943 onwards. The paints are all from Tamiya and the reference numbers are XF 64, XF 49 and XF 58.

The branches added to the chassis of the Tiger give it a touch of personality and a hint of location. They are made out of stalks and dry leaves obtained from florists' shops, stuck on with white glue mixed with water. They are then painted a green colour using an air brush and finally retouched with a brush in various shades of green plus some yellow, all to create a natural effect.

TOP **The later Tigers had an anti-aircraft machine gun.**

CENTRE **Camouflage, track links, clothing and weapons make the model more interesting.**

ABOVE **Medium-light grey was used to paint on places where the *Zimmerit* has peeled off.**

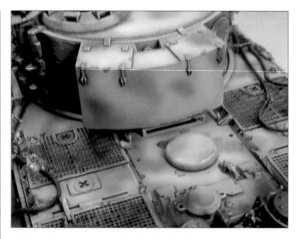

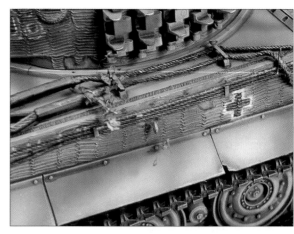

MODELLING THE STURMTIGER

LEFT **The side mudguards are cut into their different sections and then bent slightly in order to make them look more realistic.**

FAR LEFT **Hooking devices that close the toolbox also come from the etched-brass kit.**

CENTRE LEFT **The Tiger's exhaust used to leave dark stains on nearby metalwork — this is imitated using a heavily diluted black paint which is then lightly applied with an airbrush.**

FAR LEFT **The etched-brass gratings make the model more realistic and save a lot of fiddly work.**

BELOW LEFT **General view of the finished model. Usually the Tiger's paintwork stood up well to the vagaries of warfare.**

The story of this vehicle started on 9 August 1943 when Hitler suggested the manufacture of a mortar-carrier to combine the chassis of the Tiger I with the new RW61 38cm naval missile-launcher. Following a meeting with Inspector of Armoured Troops, Generaloberst Heinz Guderian, the construction of the first experimental prototype was agreed upon. Whether or not manufacturing runs for the vehicle were to be undertaken would depend upon the performance of this prototype. The decision was also taken that the chassis — a Tiger I Ausf. E — should come from the repair workshops and not from the production line. On 20 October of the same year, tests were carried out on the prototype at Arys. It was built from a chassis corresponding to the early versions of the Tiger, with rubber wheels and *Feifel* air filters. The casemate was made out of soft iron. The tests were a success, so an initial order for the manufacture of 12 units per month was placed with Alkett.

The first *38cm RW61 auf Sturmmörser Tiger* — 'Sturmtiger' or 'Sturmmörser' — had its original iron casemate replaced with another permanent one made of steel. It was sent to the Eastern Front for live combat trials, which demonstrated that it could fulfil its original requirement, namely direct support to infantry in urban battle conditions. After two months at the front it came back to Germany for improvements to be carried out with a view to its production.

RIGHT **The finished Verlinden 1/35 scale Sturmtiger.**

The size of the 38cm projectile is emphasised here.

BELOW **Front close-ups of the barrel. To the right of the gun is a hull-mounted MG34, which was made by removing the original and substituting one from Tamiya's Tiger II model. The mouth of the gun comprises an etched brass ring from On The Mark and a reinforcement made out of 2mm thick plastic card.**

However, various problems led to the project being abandoned until, in September 1944, a technical team headed by Oberst Hahne carried out repairs to the prototype that had been damaged during a bombing raid on the factory. They also completed the development of another 10 units. After congratulating the team that had carried out the work, Hitler ordered the regular production of five units and 300 projectiles per month.

By the end of 1944, Alkett had constructed a total of 12 Sturmtigers, a figure that had risen to 18 by February 1945, until another bombing raid put an end to manuacture of this vehicle. Furthermore, its production was postponed indefinitely when production of the tank that served as its base model ceased, an event

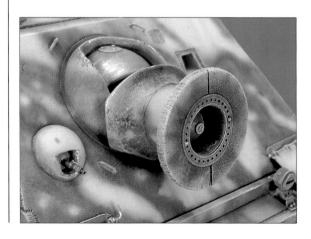

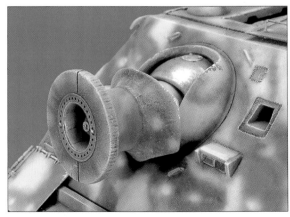

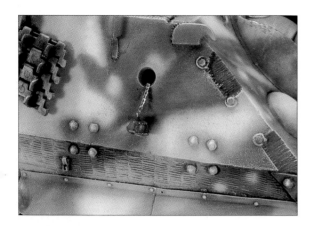

TOP **The loading crane has been completely reconstructed with the exception of part of the crank mechanism.**

TOP LEFT **On the right-hand side of the vehicle there is an opening from which the corresponding cap and chain are hanging. This served as a machine gun position for shooting from the relative safety of inside the tank.**

ABOVE AND ABOVE LEFT **We made copies of the original projectile so as to be able top get all its possible variations. One of these is seen still in its transport packing, which consisted of a wooden case sealed by two steel straps. The other has the yellow line that served as a reference mark when it was attached to the crane**

LEFT **View of the finished model.**

RIGHT AND
OPPOSITE
**Views of the
finished model.**

**BELOW It is very
easy to work on
the aluminium
sheet, which
allows you to
reproduce the
normal dents of
wear and tear on
the mudguards.**

**BOTTOM The
small attachment
points and
harnesses for the
tools are made
from etched-
brass, metal and
aluminium sheet.
The rivets on the
side aprons are
produced by
Grandt Line.**

that stimulated new research into a cheaper, lighter chassis, perhaps that of the Panther as it became clear that this machine was surplus to requirements. The Sturmtigers were assigned to the recently created Sturmkampfpanzer sAbt 1000, designed to protect the defensive Solingen-Wuppertal axis, but they were destroyed or trapped in the Ruhr basin during the month of April 1945.

Assembly

There are currently four Sturmtiger construction kits on the market — all at 1/35 scale. The Des brand version is generally of good quality and includes the Tiger I chassis; the Schmidt's kit has many defects, in contrast to the NKC kit, which is excellently made and is, perhaps, the best kit of all. However, we chose to do a conversion to an old Verlinden kit we had to show what can be done with a conversion and show the techniques involved. The Verlinden kit was not particularly good and is no longer available. Details of the pieces we used are given in the following list:

Tiger I chassis from Tamiya (ref 35146)
Mörser Verlinden Sturmtiger conversion kit
(ref 586)

WHEELS

Base: Black (XF-1 Tamiya)
    Dry brush No 62 (Humbrol)
    Dry brush No 71 (Humbrol)
    Powder airbrushed with Tamiya XF-55 and
      XF-57

TRACKS

Base: Black (XF-1 Tamiya)
    Highlights airbrushed with Tamiya XF-64,
      XF-64 and XF-3
    Dry brush No 100 and No 62 (Humbrol)
    Washes in black oils

Projections added with X-11 marker and
    Tamiya dry brush
Matt varnish from Microscale mixed in 80%
    proportion with alcohol

COLOUR RANGE

Base: 60% Tamiya XF-60,
    20% XF-2, 20% XF-3
Green: 90% Tamiya XF-58, 10% XF-3
Brown: 80% Tamiya XF-64, 20% XF-3
Dry Brush Base: Humbrol No 71 and No 74
Dry Brush Green: Humbrol HN4
Dry Brush Brown: Humbrol No 160 and No 154
Green: Moss Green Holbein (retouching)
    Grey Holbein (general shading)
Brown and rust: Burnt Sienna Holbein
    (retouching)
    Sepia Holbein (general shading)

Faber Castell chalks, natural shade 179 mixed
with black. Appearance of chipped off paint
with Humbrol no.53 and silver-based painting
using Tamiya X-11 from applied with a brush.

ABOVE **Fine aluminium sheet was used to reconstruct the mudguards, bolts and hinges. They were attached using copper wire. The light comes from Gunze Sangyo's PzIIIN.**

ABOVE **The joins between the rear and side panels have to be modified since Verlinden reproduce them the wrong way round.**

The Modelling Show etched brass (ref 007)
On The Mark etched brass (ref TMP3526),
        part No L-23R-12A-12B
Wooden bullet, 28mm diameter
Hollow aluminium tube, 15–16mm diameter
The Show Modelling Sd Kfz 7 etched-brass
        tracks (ref 013)
Light from Gunze Sangyo's PzIIIN
Tiger II machine gun barrel from Tamiya
Conical rivets (32), copied from similar parts
        from the T34/85 from Tamiya
³⁄₁₀ aluminium sheet
Antenna base taken from the Sd Kfz 251/9
        from Tamiya
Various types of rivets from Grandt Line
Periscopes (copy of the StuG IV part from
        Tamiya).

ABOVE AND OPPOSITE, BELOW
Views of the finished model.

This listing of parts is only offered as a guide, as everything depends on which spare items each modeller can get his hands on. The lights, rivets, periscopes and so on can be obtained from other model kits or, better still, by making small moulds to produce resin or metal copies. To clarify the assembly as much as possible, we have explained the modifications made to each area of the model. Our order of assembly is not important though, it is merely made for clarification.

The gun is made from an aluminium tube 15mm in diameter and 40mm in length, to which we added the armour plating from the Verlinden kit. With a mini-drill adapted to take circular sandpaper accessories, make a few rings to take an Evergreen tube 10mm in diameter and perfectly central. Instead of using the etched brass gun bore supplied in the On The Mark kit, we made a similar piece out of 0.15mm plasticard. With heat treatment we gave it a circular shape and then grooves, using the etched brass part as a reference. We then attached the ring supplied by On The Mark to the gun using superglue (US: crazy glue). The positioning of this must be perfect. Finally, we used 2mm plasticard to make another ring that, when cut in half, serves as a ring enforcement for the gun. We then added the remainder of the Verlinden parts.

To make the mudguards we used aluminium sheet — because of its resistance and ease of manipulation — making the hinges out of telephone cable and using copper wire to make the bolts for these and its covering as an addition to the casing. The butt hinges are made from identical aluminium strips, in which we made little holes for the screws. The hinges and their plates can alternatively be taken from various etched brass modelling kits.

To make the base of the light we used an aluminium strip 3mm wide, this was then attached to the chassis using four rivets. The cable for this light is threaded through the corner where the parts intersect.

Roof

This had to be almost completely reconstructed due to the poor quality of the various bits of kit. We used a mini-drill to get rid of the loading

RIGHT **General view of the completed model. Taking the etched-brass and resin Verlinden conversion kit (ref 586) and Tamiya's Tiger I kit (ref 35146) as the principal base upon which to work, we proceeded to carry out this laborious but undoubtedly spectacular transformation of the elephantine Sturmtiger.**

and access trapdoor and also hollow out the inside of the casemate. We decided to leave a hatch open so that we could add a projectile hanging from the crane. To square off the resulting hole we used 2mm strips of plasticard cut with a chamfered edge. The rear wall was sandpapered all over and the gas cylinder (which serves to help the working of the heavy shutter) was attached.

Front Section (see diagram on page 41)

We removed the barrel of the MG34 machine gun with a drill, and replaced it with another taken from a Tamiya Tiger II kit; it had to be modified slightly. We did the same thing for the main armament, hollowing out the casemate to allow for the insertion of a wooden ball. Using a circular cone bit we hollowed out the Verlinden part representing the casing of this ball.

The gun is made from an aluminium tube 15mm in diameter and 40mm in length, to which we added the armour plating from the Verlinden kit. With a mini-drill adapted to take circular sandpaper accessories, we made rings to take an Evergreen tube 10mm in diameter — making sure it was perfectly central. Instead of using the etched-brass gun bore supplied in the On The Mark kit, we then made a replacement piece out of 0.15mm plasticard, which was given a circular form by heat treatment and onto which we added grooves, using the etched-brass part as a reference. We then superglued to the gun the On The Mark ring. The positioning of this must be perfect. Finally, we used 2mm plasticard to make another ring that, cut in half, serves as a ring enforcement for the gun. Then we added the remainder of the Verlinden parts.

To make the mudguards we used aluminium sheet because it is both easy to manipulate but also retains well any shape given to it — this means that we can add wear and tear realistically. We made the

Front

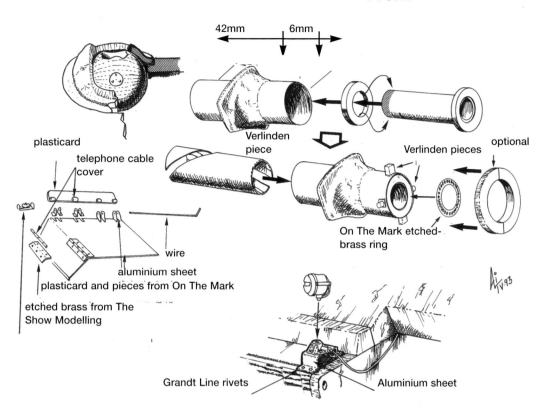

42mm

6mm

plasticard

telephone cable cover

Verlinden piece

Verlinden pieces

optional

On The Mark etched-brass ring

wire

aluminium sheet

plasticard and pieces from On The Mark

etched brass from The Show Modelling

Grandt Line rivets

Aluminium sheet

mudguard hinges out of telephone cable, using copper wire to make the bolts for these. The butt hinges are made from identical aluminium strips, in which we made holes for the screws. The hinges and their plates can also be obtained from various etched-brass modelling kits. To make the base of the light we used an aluminium strip 3mm wide that was attached to the chassis using four rivets. The cable for this light is added via the corner where the parts intersect.

Roof (see diagram on page 42)

This has to be almost completely reconstructed because of the poor quality of the elements of which it is composed. We used a mini-drill to get rid of the loading and access trapdoor and also to hollow out the inside of the casemate. We left the hatch open so that we could add a projectile hanging from the crane. To square off the resulting hole we use 2mm strips of plastic card cut with a chamfered edge. The rear wall was sandpapered all over and the gas cylinder, which helped the working of the heavy shutter, was attached.

ABOVE **The gun was built from an aluminium tube 15mm in diameter and 40mm in length. To this we added Verlinden armour plating. At a later stage the reinforcement ring will be added to the mouth of the muzzle.**

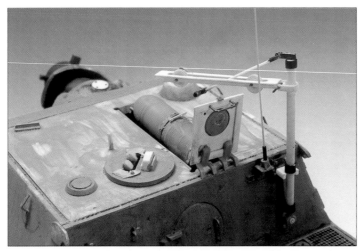

The hatches were rebuilt from 2.5mm plasticard and the frame from 0.3mm plasticard. We then added the detail as shown in the drawing (on page 43). First an inverted conical-shaped hole was made in which to insert the enclosed defence weapon so that it does not stick out. We then added a small plastic disc to this orifice; this needs to rest on the level of the internal and external surfaces. Afterwards, we added the Azimut parts and a small ring to accommodate a wing nut and six small drill holes.

The projection of the optical equipment base had to be removed so that the turret remains level — although we had to change its position since its original location was not right. To complete this part we made a 2mm thick plasticard disc, into which we drilled a few holes so that a bifocal periscope could stick out. The periscope can be taken from any other model or you can construct it yourself using strips of Evergreen and aluminium. Finally, we rectified the smoke extractor by modifying it with a mini-drill and rebuilding it according to the drawings.

TOP **view of the loading hatch.**

ABOVE **The rear panel of the casemate has been lowered by 2mm so that the sides fit onto the chassis correctly; the direction of the joins has also been corrected. The crane brackets are made using aluminium sheet, telephone cable and etched-brass wing nuts.**

Sides and rear (see diagrams on pages 43 and 45)

We removed the two original rivets and substituted different ones as indicated in the list of materials (see page 39). The direction of the joins on the rear panel of the casemate has to be inverted since Verlinden put them the wrong way round. The rear panel and the side panels of the body had to be lowered by 2mm so that the sides fitted onto the chassis correctly. Using 1.5mm plasticard we cut a small curved piece corresponding to the part of the turret ring that sticks out beneath the casemate (see centre photograph on page 44 for a good view of this). The crane brackets were made out of aluminium and decorated with etched-brass wing nuts and copper wire. The lower bracket can be made out of a single conical cylinder or, alternatively, two tubes inserted one inside the other.

Except for the crank mechanism the projectile lifting crane had to be completely rebuilt. The small wheels were made from three pieces of plasticard sandpapered to shape as necessary. The crane was built from scored Evergreen plasticard; make the slot first and then extract the part carefully avoid any mis-shaping. Sandpaper was then used to eliminate

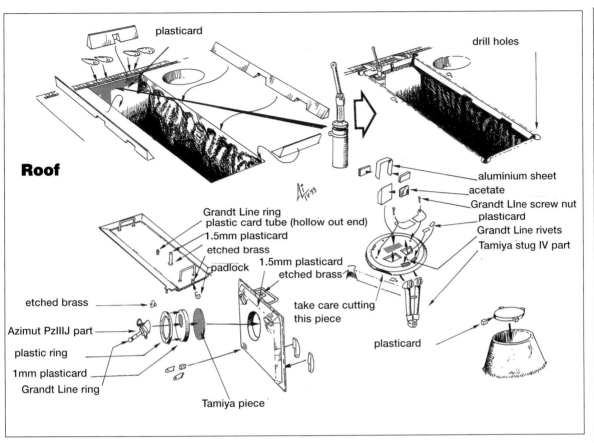

Roof

plasticard

drill holes

aluminium sheet
acetate
Grandt LIne screw nut
plasticard
Grandt Line rivets
Tamiya stug IV part

Grandt Line ring
plastic card tube (hollow out end)
1.5mm plasticard
etched brass
padlock

1.5mm plasticard
etched brass

take care cutting
this piece

plasticard

etched brass

Azimut PzIIIJ part

plastic ring

1mm plasticard

Grandt Line ring

Tamiya piece

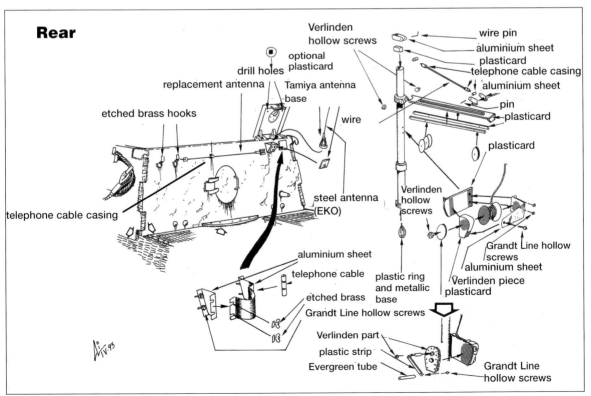

Rear

Verlinden
hollow screws

wire pin
aluminium sheet
plasticard
telephone cable casing
aluminium sheet
pin
plasticard

optional
plasticard

drill holes

replacement antenna

Tamiya antenna
base

etched brass hooks

wire

plasticard

telephone cable casing

steel antenna
(EKO)

Verlinden
hollow
screws

Grandt Line hollow
screws
aluminium sheet
Verlinden piece
plasticard

aluminium sheet

telephone cable

plastic ring
and metallic
base

etched brass

Grandt Line hollow screws

Verlinden part

plastic strip

Evergreen tube

Grandt Line
hollow screws

the scoring. The upper brace was made from wire and telephone cable casing and its supports from aluminium and plasticard. For the mechanism, we used the one provided by Verlinden, but separated its two parts with a plastic strip that attaches the whole mechanism to the mast. The roller that controls the cable was made using the same method as with the small wheels, taking into account the fact that its centre is tubular.

On the two sides of the body we used parts from The Modelling Show for the tool attachments and harnesses, as shown in the diagrams. Then, using aluminium, we had to make the front mudguard on each side as the ones on this vehicle are longer than those on the Tiger I.

On the rear part of the body we attached etched-brass pieces as indicated and added the block of wood for the clamp, together with the small bolts that can be seen at the top and bottom of the part located between the two exhaust pipes.

Projectiles

We made copies of the one projectile supplied by the manufacturer. This was in order to show all the different possible uses that can be made of the projectiles. Accordingly, we showed one with the metal bracket that attached it to the crane, and on the other we have painted the yellow line that served as a reference mark for attachment purposes. The third version incorporated its transport packaging which comprises a casing of wooden strips held in place by two steel belts (see diagrams).

OPPOSITE, TOP **The side skirts, rivets and attachments are added onto the sides of the vehicle. The first mudguard on each side has also been especially built.**

OPPOSITE, CENTRE **The etched-brass metal grilles supplied by Tamiya for the Tiger I are placed on top of the ventilation intakes.**

OPPOSITE, BOTTOM **The etched-brass parts, the wooden block for the clamp and the bolts for the part located between the two exhaust pipes are placed on the rear panel of the body.**

LEFT **Side of casemate showing side skirts.**

Sides

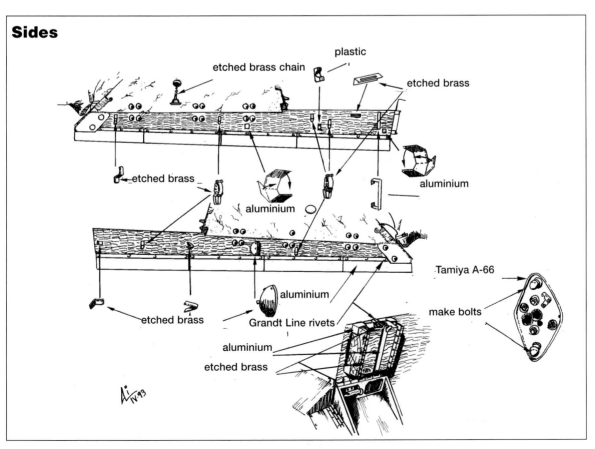

plastic

etched brass chain

etched brass

etched brass

aluminium

etched brass

aluminium

aluminium

etched brass

Grandt Line rivets

aluminium

etched brass

Tamiya A-66

make bolts

WALKROUND

1 Front of the Tiger I at Saumur Museum, France. Note open hatches on hull front for driver (right) and radio operator/machine gunner (left).

2 Main 8.8cm Kwk 36 L/56 gun mounting and coaxial MG34 port.

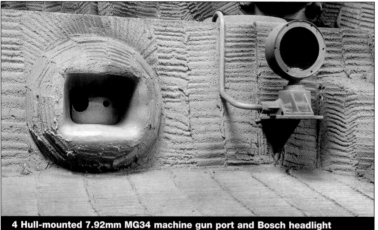

4 Hull-mounted 7.92mm MG34 machine gun port and Bosch headlight detail. Note *Zimmerit*.

5 Turret side detail.

7 Back of left drive sprocket. Note hole for towing hook.

8 Turret top (40mm of armour plate) — note commander's cupola with periscopes and loader's hatch and periscope (nearest camera).

3 Mantlet and Bosch headlight detail.

6 Driver's hatch detail. Note hook for hanging track cable.

9 Open driver's hatch detail. Note periscope block.

KEY TO WALKROUND

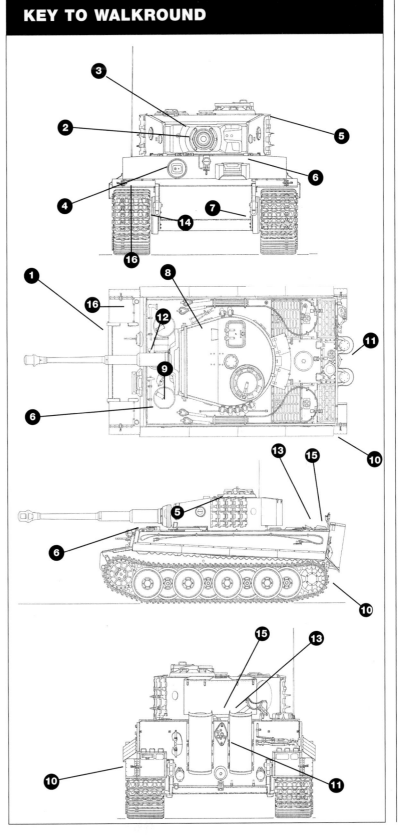

10 Track, idler sprocket and interlocking roadwheel detail.

11 Exhaust stack detail (note no heat shields).

12 Front hull air filter and rear of Bosch headlight.

13 Rear deck detail: fuel filler cap (x on top) near camera.

14 Track detail. Battle tracks could be as wide as 725mm.

15 Cap for snorkel and exhaust stack.

16 Access to front drive sprocket afforded by raising mudguard.

Early production Tiger I of 503rd SPzAbt, July 1943. Note rear *Feifel* air filters.

Mid-production Tiger I of 506th SPzAbt, 1944.

Late production Tiger I of SS-PzAbt101; Obersturmführer Wittmann's tank in 1944.

SCALE DRAWINGS

EARLY PRODUCTION VERSION
Length: 8.45m
Width: 3.7m
Height: 2.93m
Weight: 57 tons
Speed: 38km/hr
Engine: Maybach HL210 P45
Endurance: 140km
Crew: Commander; driver;
machine gunner/radio-operator;
gunner; loader
Weapons: 1 x 8.8cm KwK36
L/56; 2 x 7.92mm MG34
Ammunition: 92 main gun, 4,800
MG rounds

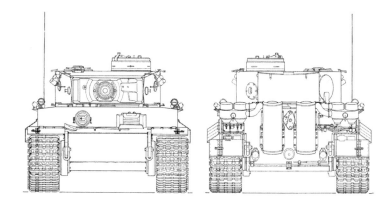

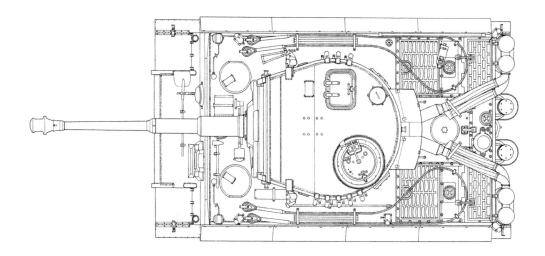

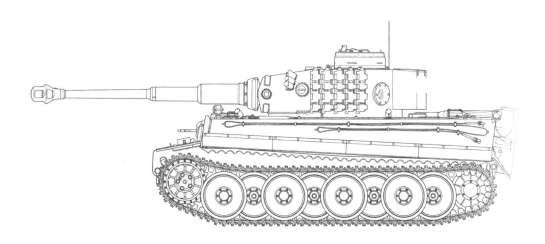

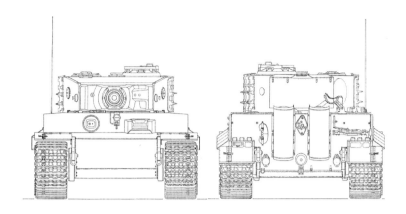

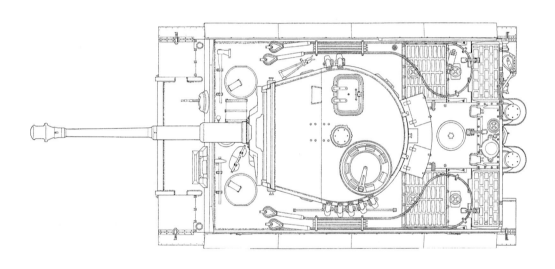

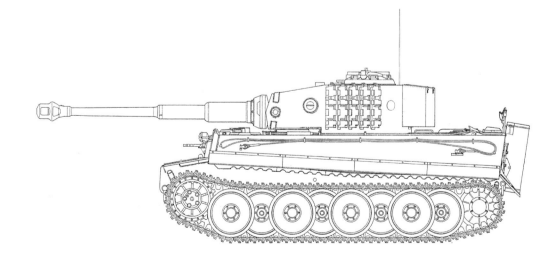

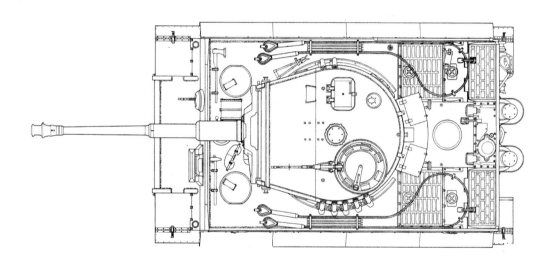

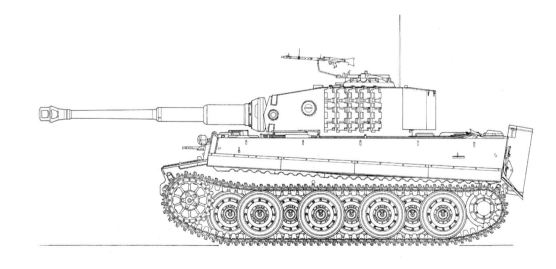

STURMTIGER
Length: 6.28m
Width: 3.57m
Height 2.58m
Weight 66.045kg
Speed: 45.4km/h
Engine: Maybach HL210 P45
Endurance: 100/60km
Crew: Commander; driver;
machine gunner/radio-operator;
gunner; loader
Weapons: 1 x 38cm Stu M61
L/5.4; 1 x 7.92mm MG34
Ammunition: 14 x 38cm; 2,500 x
7.92mm

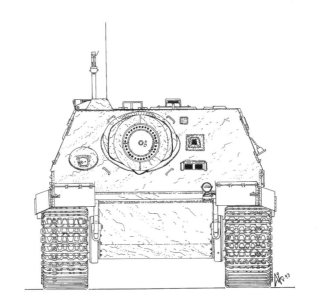

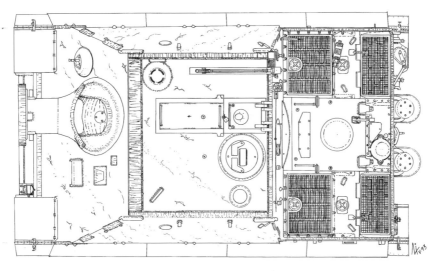

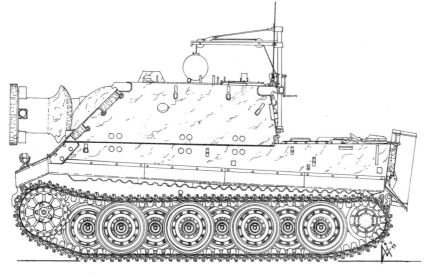

CAMOUFLAGE AND MARKINGS

CAMOUFLAGE COLOURS AND PATTERNS

Modelling the Tiger gives you the opportunity to choose from a wide range of camouflage colours and schemes. In the early years of World War Two German armour was mainly painted in plain grey, sometimes with brown bands added over it. Though there is evidence that in 1939-40 the grey was extremely dark — almost an off-black rather than a grey — by 1942 it seems to have become slightly lighter and can be matched reasonably well by the 'panzer grey' or 'tank grey' from many model paint ranges. By this time the bands of brown seem to have disappeared, so the first Tigers on the Leningrad Front were painted in plain grey.

At almost the same time, Tigers were being shipped to Tunisia for the Afrika Korps' last stand. There's still a great deal of debate about their colour scheme, but photographs of them being delivered to their Batallions and of their loading on the ships which carried them across the Mediterranean Sea show a fairly light single tone, which must have been a sand colour. Several variations of 'Afrika Korps sand' are available in model paint ranges, corresponding to the several known versions of sand colour used by the Germans, and the choice of which to use is up to the modeller since none has yet been proved to be that used on Tigers. The sand colour may also have been used on the second batch of Tigers sent to Russia.

While in Tunisia some Tigers seem to have been overpainted in a green colour of unknown shade. Some references indicate a pea-green while others state specifically that captured US olive drab was used. Again, there is no definite evidence so the modeller's choice is free until some evidence is found and published.

ABOVE **Typical mottled finish of green and brown spots and stripes sprayed onto a dark yellow base coat.**

RIGHT **This Tiger shows a subtle brown mottle over the basic dark yellow.**

OPPOSITE, ABOVE **Idiosyncratic battalion markings for 506 sPzAbt (see page 22).**

OPPOSITE, BELOW **Tiger 322 (the second tank in the 2nd Platoon of the 3rd Company. Note 507 sPzAbt tactical marking to left of bucket on rear of tank.**

CAMOUFLAGE COLOURS AND PATTERNS

The pattern Zimmerit makes when applied to flat surfaces is completely different to that applied elsewhere.

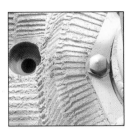

This photograph of the Tiger at Saumur illustrates well the pattern of *Zimmerit* applied to curved or rounded surfaces.

Crews interpreted camouflage instructions differently. The photos above and above left and show how different green stripes can look.

Typical 'ambush' pattern camouflage with small spots of the base, yellow, colour sprayed onto a green and brown background.

Some of the Tigers intended for use in Tunisia were too late to serve there and went instead to Sicily. Their colour was probably the sand shade used in Africa. Further Tiger deliveries went to units in Italy and may also have been that same colour.

A new camouflage scheme was introduced from mid-1943. This used the shade known as *dunkelgelb*, or panzer yellow, as a base coat and was intended to be overpainted by troops in the field with red-brown and green as required to match local terrain and foliage. The exact colour of *dunkelgelb* remains a matter of intense debate, so the paints offered in model ranges can be used according to the modeller's personal choice. The red-brown and green were supplied as a paste and were diluted by the troops with whatever was handy. Since neither the dilutant nor the amount of dilution was standard the resulting colours varied widely, from very pale to rather dark and also in shade of brown and green. The patterns varied as widely, from sprayed rolling bands of a single colour to complicated three-colour schemes which were often applied with paintbrushes to give hard edges to the colours. Some Tigers remained in plain *dunkelgelb* until, like those in the grey or sand schemes, they were repainted when a unit was out of combat.

During the winters of 1942/43 and 1943/44 a white coat was used on the Russian Front. This varied from a quickly smeared job, using ordinary whitewash and applied by any means to hand from paintbrushes to brooms and even rags dipped in paint, to a very smart pure white coat applied with a spraygun and covering the whole tank evenly. Gaps were sometimes left in the white to let the unit markings and tactical numbers remain visible. White camouflage does not seem to have been much used on the Western Front or in Italy.

MARKINGS

All Tigers carried the the standard German cross, the Balkankreuz, as a national identity marking. This was usually on the hull side but sometimes on the turret side instead, or as well, and on the stowage box mounted on the back of the turret.

Three-digit tactical numbers were usually used, indicating from left to right the company, platoon and individual tank. They were usually on the turret sides, sometimes on the back of the turret stowage bin as well, but at least one unit put them on the gun recoil sleeve instead. Black, red and blue were fairly common and outlines in white or yellow were often added to them. Some Tigers carried white numbers, and others used dashed outlines without coloured centres instead of solid numbers.

Unit markings varied quite widely, from small tactical symbols to colourful and proudly displayed heraldic badges. Their placing was equally varied — for instance small white rhomboids appeared on the forward hull sides of one Tiger unit in Tunisia while the other Tiger unit there carried a full-colour stalking tiger above the drivers visors of its tanks. In Russia the unit badges were frequently carried on the turret-rear stowage box, but one batallion moved its tactical numbers to the gun recoil sleeve to make room for a charging knight on horseback on the turret side. This isn't the place for a list of badges and the units which carried them, but many are illustrated in New Vanguard 5 on the Tiger I and others can be found in the references listed later.

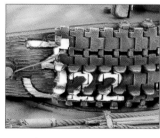

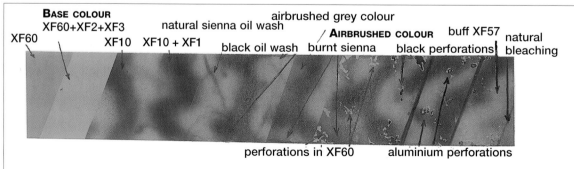

ABOVE AND LEFT **Examples of tactical markings on turret sides and rear. Note the way the marking has been included on the track links.**

BASE COLOUR
XF60+XF2+XF3
XF60
XF10   XF10 + XF1

natural sienna oil wash
black oil wash

airbrushed grey colour
AIRBRUSHED COLOUR
burnt sienna

buff XF57
black perforations

natural bleaching

perforations in XF60   aluminium perforations

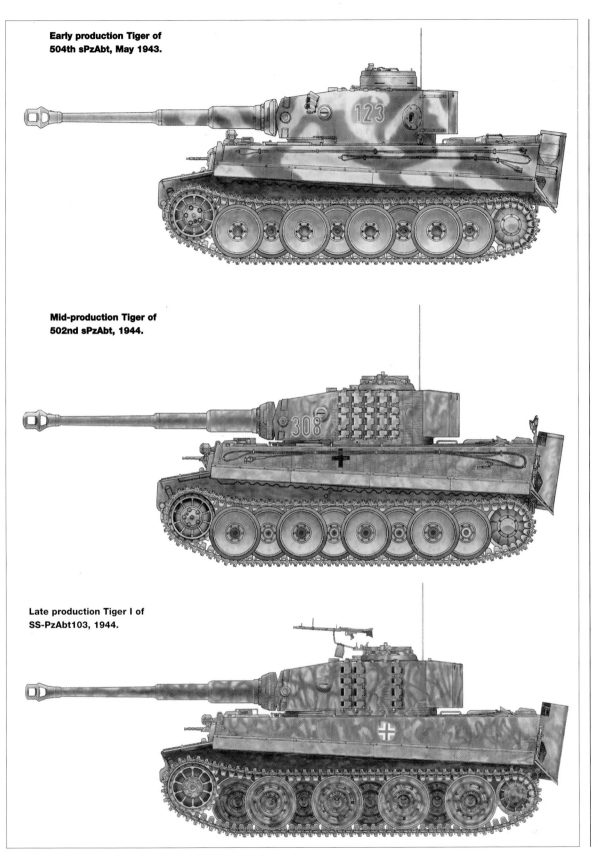

**Early production Tiger of
504th sPzAbt, May 1943.**

**Mid-production Tiger of
502nd sPzAbt, 1944.**

**Late production Tiger I of
SS-PzAbt103, 1944.**

MODEL ROUNDUP

As mentioned in the Introduction, there are quite a few Tiger I kits available in various scales, and manufacturers have produced a variety of accessories, upgrades and conversion kits to go with them. Although space doesn't allow an exhaustive list, the following are the most easily available.

Unlike the kits, accessory and upgrade sets can be hard to find. Study the advertisements in the model magazines published in your country for stockists outside the UK.

Aber makes a range of etched metal accessories which includes many sets for the Tiger I. 35015 is for the basic Tiger tank and gives engine deck grilles, tools, clasps, stowage brackets which can be made to work, and many other small detail parts. 35043 and 35047 are exterior and interior detail sets for the Sturmtiger and should fit both the Tamiya and Italeri kits. Aber also make smaller sets with fewer parts, and here 35A10 gives the front and rear folding trackguards, 35A11 the side trackguards fitted to very early Tigers, 35A12 the standard side trackguards, and 35A13 those for the Italeri Porsche Tiger, while 35A43 is side track-guards as fitted to the Sturmtiger and ABG03 is a simple set of engine deck grilles. All are *** rating for quality but only the trackguard and engine deck grille sets are rated 'A' as suitable for beginners, the others being rated 'B' as some experience with etched metal will be needed to handle their smaller parts. The UK agent is Historex Agents, telephone 01304 206720, email Sales@historex-agents.co.uk.

Anvil Productions has a range of simply superb Tiger I accessory sets. Snap-together resin link-to-link tracks are available for the early and late Tigers, and are engineered to need only minimal cleanup and give really easy assembly. They can also be had with extra parts to complete details which Tamiya and/or Italeri couldn't provide due to moulding limitations, but these need a little care in handling so are more for moderately-experienced modellers. Made in Australia but not yet exported to any overseas agent so you need a pen-friend there to help you get them — but well worth the effort. Ratings: tracks *** A, extra parts *** B.

Armoured Brigade Models produces two Tiger I turrets with correct shapes to replace the incorrect ones given in most kits. Both late and mid-production versions are available and are really excellent. Rating *** B. Accurate Armour is the UK agent for ABM, telephone 01475 743955, email enquiries@accurate-armour.com.

Eduard is another etched metal set maker with products for the Tiger I. Their set 35085 is for the Sturmtiger and 35131 specifically for Tamiya's mid-production Tiger. 35133 gives exterior and 35134 interior details for the Academy Tiger kits, 35219 for Italeri's Bergetiger, and 35232 for Italeri's Porsche Tiger. Set 35301 is for Tamiya's early Tiger I and 35305 for the Italeri kit. Like the Aber sets, all are *** for quality but

KITS (all polystyrene except where indicated)

Maker	Variant	Rating
½₂ scale		
Airfix	late production	* A
½₂ scale		
Revell	Early production as used in Tunisia	*** A
⅑₅ scale		
Academy	Early production, includes many interior parts	*** B
"	Mid production	
⅑₅ scale		
Italeri	Porsche Tiger	** B
"	Initial production as used in Tunisia, labelled as Ausf E/H1	** B
"	Sturmtiger, includes interior parts	*** B
"	Bergetiger	** B
⅑₅ scale		
Tamiya	Initial production, labelled as Afrika Korps, has the correct turret shape	*** A
"	Early production, has the correct turret shape	*** A
"	Mid production	*** A
"	Late production, also available with special decals	*** A
"	Sturmtiger, includes interior parts	*** A
½₅ scale		
Tamiya	Early production, includes many interior parts	** B
⅟₆ scale		
Tamiya	Just announced, radio controlled model with many operating functions including gun and engine sound effects. Expected to be	*** B
Verlinden	Late production. This is a resin kit	** C
"	Sturmtiger. Resin kit	** C

KEY

Symbol	Meaning
***	a top quality kit
**	medium quality
*	less detailed
A	simple enough for a beginner to build successfully
B	suitable for moderately experienced modellers
C	for experts only

Note: the marking of kits and accessories as simple enough for a beginner is not intended to devalue them in expert eyes, just to show which ones inexperienced modellers can tackle and still produce good results.

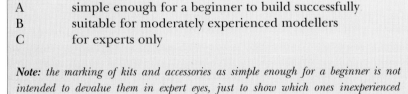

experience is needed to handle their smaller parts — so rated A for the engine grilles, trackguards and other larger bits that everyone can use and B for those little bits. If you can't find them locally, the UK agent is LSA Models, telephone 01273 705420, email lsamodels@mc.mail.com.

Friulimodel offers white metal link-to-link tracks for the Tiger I. ALT06 is the basic battle track set, ALT25 are the early-type tracks and ALT26 are the narrow transport tracks. All are easy to use and the weight of their metal gives them a very true-to-life drape across the Tiger's wheel layout. The original sets used 'claws' cast into the links which are pressed closed to hold track pins cast into the adjoining links, but these are gradually being replaced by remoulded types which have holes cast for track pins which are cut from the soft wire provided. Both types are easy to use, but you should be aware that the early type can come stretched or even undone under their own weight. Rating *** A. Available from Historex Agents in the UK.

Jordi Rubio is an established maker of turned aluminium gun barrels, which simply replace the plastic parts, and produces one for the Tiger I. If you have difficulties cleaning up the long joints of two-part polystyrene gun barrels without losing their round shape these are worth using instead; they are available from USA Models in the United Kingdom. Rating *** A.

Model Kasten of Japan also has link-to-link track sets for Tigers.

MK04 is a set that you glue together and drape round the wheels before the glue sets completely, while MSK01, 02 and 03 are working late, early and transport tracks respectively. The working sets are assembled, on a jig (provided), by gluing plastic pins into holes already made in the links just like real track pins. MSK04 and 05 are late and early spare track links for stowing on your model. All these are polystyrene. MA08 is a set to build a drum cupola with internal details and MW01 is a set of nicely detailed early Tiger I road wheels — useful to replace the Italeri ones if you don't like their detail but do want the *Zimmerit* finish of that kit. Rating: *** A. Accurate Armour is the UK agent for Model Kasten.

Royal Model of Italy has several sets using resin and etched metal to upgrade the Tiger and Sturmtiger. Their quality is generally good but they are hard to find. Rating ** B.

Tamiya offers an etched metal set of engine deck grilles for all of its Tiger I kits. Since all Tigers had these grilles it is well worth getting for your model even if you don't want to add any other aftermarket details. Most good model shops will have these for sale. Rating *** A.

The Tank Workshop has some useful Tiger I sets. One which seems to be out of production is a complete interior for fighting compartment and engine bay, which is well worth grabbing if you find it anywhere. Still available are sets 2039, a 'partial' interior which gives the bits that can be seen through the turret and hull hatches, 2050, a canvas-covered muzzle brake for the early and mid-production Tigers, and 2051 which is the same but for the late production Tiger. Rating *** A for the covered muzzle brakes and *** B for the interior set. LSA Models is the UK agent.

Verlinden Productions have a small range of useful Tiger items in resin. Item 526 is a Tiger I engine compartment, 1177 is an exterior detail set and includes etched metal details, 1250 is a stick-on *Zimmerit* set which you can use instead of modelling *Zimmerit* yourself, 1360 is a disassembled Tiger I engine, 1370 is a complete late Tiger I rear compartment giving not just the engine bay but fuel tanks and radiators as well, and 1462 is a stick-on *Zimmerit* set for the Sturmtiger and includes etched metal trackguards. All these are ⅟₃₅ scale, designed for the Tamiya kits but usable for the Italeri ones as well. Rating *** B.

In ⅟₆ scale Verlinden has a stick-on *Zimmerit* set and an engine compartment for its Tiger I kit, plus a Sturmtiger conversion. Rating ** B. Larger model shops often stock the Verlinden range, but you can also mail-order from Historex Agents in the UK and from many stockists in other countries.

REFERENCES

BIBLIOGRAPHY

The best single reference for the Tiger I is New Vanguard 5, *Tiger I Heavy Tank 1942-1945* by Tom Jentz and Hilary Doyle (ISBN 185532-337-0, Osprey, 1993). This is much more than a superb potted history of the tank's development, but also includes a summary of use by each unit with many photos and excellent colour plates by Peter Sarsons accompanied by comprehensive notes on the camouflage colours and markings shown.

Messrs Jentz and Doyle have also produced a much fuller three-volume work on the Tigers. Although Volume 3 covers the Tiger B, or King Tiger, Volume 1 covers the tank's development from A to Z in much more detail than was possible in their New Vanguard book and Volume 2 goes into great detail on tactics and service use. These two books are expensive, but if you want really detailed information with a splendid collection of in-service and detail close-up photographs they're well worth getting. Volume 1's ISBN is 0-7643-1038-0, published 2000, and Volume 2's is 0-7643-0225-6, published 1997, and both are published by Schiffer Publishing Ltd.

Tigers In Combat is by Wolfgang Scheider and covers exactly what it says in the title. Masses of photographs of Tigers in unit service show their camouflage and markings, colour plates by Jean Restayn interpret these, and there are unit histories which include long extracts from the day-to-day battle diaries. Volume 1 covers all the numbered Army Tiger units, and Volume 2 deals with the SS units and various battle groups. Again, they're expensive but worth the money, and you can always obtain them through inter-library lending services. Volume 1 (ISBN 0-921991-21-5) was published 1994 but has been revised and reprinted as this book was in preparation; Volume 2 has ISBN 0-921991-39-8.

Uwe Feist's and Bruce Culver's *Tiger I* gives much information about the Tiger's development and combat use, with excellent photographs. This was a limited edition, so grab it if you see it for sale.

Culver and Feist produced *Tiger I And Sturmtiger In Detail*, which contains many close-up photographs as its name indicates.

Also *Panzer Colours 3* and many photos in general books on German armour.

TIGERS IN MUSEUMS

The Tank Museum at Bovington, a few miles north of Bournemouth on the South Coast of England, has an early production Tiger — actually the first one to be captured. It is under restoration to running condition at the moment so may not be on public display, although the turret was accessible in 1999, but the Museum library has a superb collection of photographs of it as well as of other Tigers.

The Musée des Blindes at Saumur in France, an easy train ride from Paris, has a late production Tiger I. If you plan to visit, ask in advance whether photography will be permitted as conditions of admission seem to vary. The latest reports are that photography has been banned, but this couldn't be confirmed at the time of writing.

Also in France is a very late production Tiger I at Vimoutiers, near Lisieux in Normandy. This is by the roadside and easy to access, so although its not in pristine condition it's well worth a visit if you're in that area.

The famous Russian tank museum at Kublinka also has a late Tiger I. This is not the easiest museum in the world to visit, so joining a pre-organised tour is the best way to go.

Another early Tiger I captured in Tunisia by the US Army, was for many years on display at Aberdeen Proving Ground in Maryland. It was sent several years ago to Germany for restoration, but this project appears to have fallen through and the last reports were that it had gone to an undisclosed location in England for work to be done.

TIGER WEBSITES

There are several excellent Tiger websites for those with access to the Web. Bovington Tank Museum has a site dedicated to the Tiger I restoration at http://www.tiger-tank.com, with photographs and a discussion group. The Saumur Museum's Tiger I is given good coverage at http://tiger1e.com/saumur, with photographs of its interior.

That last site is actually accessible direct from the Tiger I site run by David Bryden, a Tiger fan who is constructing a very valuable reference site at http://tiger1e.com. As well as links to the Bovington and Saumur sites he includes detailed CAD drawings of various components.

Several tank discussion groups on the web are worth a visit too, where you're welcome to pose questions and get answers from the groups — which include many renowned modellers and Tiger students.

Missing Links is at http://missing-lynx.com/, Track-Link at http://www.track-link.net/, AFV News at http://www.mo-money.com/AFV-news/, and Hyperscale at http://www.hyperscale.com. Genuine enquiries are welcome at all of these.

Other discussion groups and reference sites exist, far too many to list here but links to them can be found at Tony Matelliano's Scale Model Links, a superb site giving links to all kinds of modelling web resources. It's at http://www.buffnet.net/~tonym/models.htm.